Cultivating Knowledge, Building Language

Cultivating Knowledge, Building Language

Literacy Instruction for English Learners in Elementary School

NONIE K. LESAUX • JULIE RUSS HARRIS

HEINEMANN
Portsmouth, NH

Heinemann
361 Hanover Street
Portsmouth, NH 03801–3912
www.heinemann.com

Offices and agents throughout the world

Library of Congress Cataloging-in-Publication Data
Lesaux, Nonie K.
Cultivating knowledge, building language : literacy instruction for English learners in elementary school / Nonie K. Lesaux and Julie Russ Harris.
pages cm—(The Research-Informed Classroom)
Includes bibliographical references and index.
ISBN 978-0-325-06250-1
1. English language—Study and teaching (Elementary)—Foreign speakers. 2. English language—Study and teaching (Elementary). 3. Literacy—Study and teaching (Elementary). 4. Education, Bilingual. 5. Language acquisition. I. Harris, Julie Russ. II. Title.

PE1128.A2L387 2015
372.652′1044—dc23 2014049752

Editor: Zoë Ryder White
Production: Vicki Kasabian
Interior design: Shawn Girsberger
Cover design: Suzanne Heiser
Cover photograph: Blend Images–KidStock/Getty Images
Typesetter: Shawn Girsberger
Manufacturing: Steve Bernier

Printed in the United States of America on acid-free paper
23 22 21 20 19 VP 3 4 5 6

To the many students, teachers, and instructional leaders with whom we have been fortunate enough to work with over the years. Your tireless commitment to learning sustains and inspires our own.

Contents

Message from Nell K. Duke

We all know that the number of students in the U.S. whose home language is not English is enormous. These students deserve our very best instruction. But what *is* the very best instruction for English learners? How do we capitalize on and further develop the linguistic knowledge and skill of this segment of our society?

Nonie Lesaux and Julie Harris are exceedingly well qualified to address these questions. They are on the cutting edge of instruction for English learners. Their combination of research knowledge and practical experience makes for guidance that can be trusted, and implemented, in classrooms throughout the country.

The overall approach that Nonie and Julie present can be summarized in two words: *big* and *deep*. They call for structuring the curriculum for English learners around content-rich big ideas—for example, how seasons influence living things, how regions of the United States contribute to our union, effecting change in our school. Then they invite teachers and students to go deep into these ideas, studying a small set of words intensely, developing great facility with a small set of word-learning strategies, and developing projects in which students demonstrate the considerable expertise they have developed.

This approach makes sense for English learners, given what we know about common strengths and needs of this group. But it also makes sense for all learners. My own children's home language is English, and yet I couldn't help but think how wonderful Nonie and Julie's approach would be for them. Indeed, many practices described in this book, while particularly important and well-suited for English learners, can be beneficial for monolingual English speakers as well.

This book fits beautifully in the Research-Informed Classroom series, which aims to bring rigorous classroom-based research to bear on persistent challenges of classroom practice. This series aims to bridge the gap between research and practice by focusing on the most practical, classroom-relevant research and communicating practices based on that research in a way that makes them accessible, appealing, and actionable. The series is founded on the belief that students and teachers are researchers' clients, and serving them should be the highest priority. I cannot thank Nonie and Julie enough for exemplifying the ideals of the series.

Nell K. Duke

University of Michigan

Acknowledgments

This book has benefited immeasurably from the collaboration, intellectual investment, and encouragement of many individuals. Because most of the ideas featured in the book grew out of the ALIAS project, our first round of thanks goes to our partners in the San Diego Unified School District, the members of that project team, and the organizations that made the project possible by awarding Nonie the funds to put her vision into action (the Institute of Education Sciences, the William T. Grant Foundation, and the William and Flora Hewlett Foundation). A very special thanks to the teachers who brought the strategies featured in this book to life each day in their classrooms and allowed us to examine their impact on teaching and learning, as well as the students who worked so hard to meet the challenges their teachers put forward. We are also indebted to Carol Barry, Terry Walter, and Jennifer Cheatham for their partnership, championing the project both for the benefit of their own district and for the field at large. Without a doubt, we are incredibly grateful to entire project team: Joan Kelley, Michael Kieffer, Andrea Anushko, Phoebe Sloane, Taralynn Kantor, Amy Griffiths, Mark Nielsen, Tisha Ruibal, Sean Preci, Greta Castaneda, Beth Faller, and Michelle Hastings, owing special thanks to Joan Kelley for intellectual contributions and her tireless work developing the curriculum, and to

Michael Kieffer—this book engages his scholarship and the middle school ESL teacher he is at his core. So many of the ideas we outline here were shaped through collaboration with Joan and Michael.

We are also very grateful to the team members who worked on the longitudinal study of reading development among Spanish-speaking English language learners from early childhood through early adolescence, and to the Eunice Kennedy Shriver National Institute of Child Health and Human Development for the funding. The study's findings were the impetus for our collective press for instructional and intervention work—the instructional strategies described in this book. Specifically, a big thanks to Jeannette Mancilla-Martinez given her instrumental role in that study, intellectually and practically, and to Armida Lizarraga, for her dedication to the project, including years of coordinating annual field-based data collection—one student at a time.

And today, at Harvard, we are continually afforded the good fortune of the ideas and thinking of those in the Language Diversity and Literacy Development Research Group: Mary Burkhauser, Emily Phillips Galloway, Robin Kane, Rebecca Lebowitz, Sky Marietta, and Rebecca Givens Rolland. We greatly appreciated all the ways in which you supported the development of this book—from feedback on chapters, to brainstorming content, to encouragement and support during the crunch.

Thanks to Zoë White at Heinemann, who stewarded this project throughout the publication process, and great thanks to Nell Duke, for inviting and encouraging us to contribute to this series.

Finally, we are indebted to family and friends, whose support and cheerleading was instrumental in bringing this book to fruition. Nonie thanks Scott for his genuine partnership day to day, and she thanks Morgan for the daily reminder of the language-knowledge connection and the power of conversation for the developing mind. Julie thanks Nick for his patience and genuine interest in discussing even the most minute details of the book, his delicious Friday night dinners, and for his unfailing belief in the project. She is also grateful to her parents, Debbie and George, who have always cultivated her knowledge and courage; special thanks to Debbie, for "the plan."

1

What We Know About Reading Development Among English Learners

Just after the bell had rung to signal the end of lunch, Ms. Parkin, a third-grade teacher, was entering the building for the first time that day. She had spent the morning in a training session—the second one in a series of three—focused on strengthening daily instruction for English learners (ELs). With almost forty different home languages in the district today, and the population increasing each year, the district had begun to offer trainings for all teachers of ELs, not just English as a second language (ESL) teachers, on how to support language development. In Ms. Parkin's classroom this year, more than half of the students are ELs—some are receiving ESL services, some have been reclassified as fully proficient, but all need language support. Ms. Parkin can think back to a time, not too long ago, when she had just one, maybe two ELs in her classroom per year, and before that, none.

English Learners in Today's Schools

Ms. Parkin's experience in her district is not a unique one. In industrialized countries worldwide, the population of children growing up in linguistically diverse homes is on the rise (UNICEF Innocenti Research Centre 2009). In fact, over half of the world's population is now bilingual, and in today's globalized economy, the ability to speak more than one language is an enormous asset (Grosjean

2010). In the United States in particular, the past several decades have seen a dramatic increase in the number of school-age children from homes where English is not the primary language. Between 1980 and 2009, this population of children, ELs, rose from 4.7 to 11.2 million youth, or from 10 to 21 percent of school-age children (Aud et al. 2011). Approximately 73 percent of ELs come from households in which Spanish is the primary language spoken, but the remainder of the population speaks 150 other languages at home (Batalova and McHugh 2010).

As we think more and more scientifically about the needs of this population, it is important to recognize that although one might hear the term *English learner* and conjure up the notion of a recent immigrant, more than half of school-age ELs are born in the United States. In fact, the two largest and fastest growing subpopulations of U.S. ELs are students who immigrated before kindergarten and U.S.-born children of immigrants (Capps et al. 2005)—they are not newcomers, enrolling as older children and adolescents. Instead, they are in our preschools and kindergarten classrooms, being educated entirely in the United States. These learners are coming up through the system—and their families have high hopes for their children's education. After all, when immigrant adults are asked about their reasons for immigration to the United States, there is one resounding reason that is at the very top, each and every time. What is it? A better education and life—not for them, but for their children. This is at the root of most every immigrant family's plan. They embark on the difficult, even traumatic, process of abandoning their homeland, and they take on the enormous task of learning life in a new country. These undertakings are commenced and continued, not for themselves, but instead, with the next generation(s) in mind (Perreira, Chapman, and Stein 2006). Immigrant parents enroll their young children in early education and care settings and kindergarten classrooms and think favorably about the U.S. public education system. These families often associate the United States with better opportunities and a better life for the next generation, based on education and schooling (Goldenberg et al. 2001; Perreira, Chapman, and Stein 2006).

Yet although many ELs in the United States thrive academically, when compared to their majority-culture peers, this population on average demonstrates lower academic achievement, experiences grade retention, and drops out of school at higher rates (August and Hakuta 1997; August and Shanahan 2006; Fry 2007; Snow, Burns, and Griffin 1998). Large-scale assessment results confirm the troubling demographics of reading difficulties in the United States. For example, according to the 2013 National Assessment of Educational Progress results, only 7 percent of students classified as English language learners in grade 4 and 3 percent in grade 8 read at or above proficiency levels (National Center for Education

Statistics 2013). And bear in mind that these comparisons do not represent the very large proportion of the population that was never identified as needing language supports or that was reclassified as fully proficient; it is unclear, then, how the overall population of ELs is faring.

Although there are many risk factors associated with academic outcomes, many of which ELs carry with them, one risk factor is unique to this population: Its members are faced with the challenge of simultaneously learning academic content and developing English language proficiency, and they have to learn with enormous efficiency to catch up with their monolingual English peers. Without a doubt, this task is a formidable one. ELs are racing the clock and the calendar, and their teachers are working tirelessly to support them to do so.

We have a long way to go to fully serve this fast-growing group, now populating classrooms across the country. The opportunity gap between ELs and many of their peers is too wide, high school graduation rates are still too low, and

HOW DOES POVERTY FIT INTO THE PICTURE?

At the same time as having to learn to read in a language in which they are not fully proficient, other risk factors associated with the EL population include household incomes at or near poverty levels; low parental education and literacy rates; and enrollment in under-resourced, low-performing schools with high concentrations of students of color and students living in poverty (Aud et al. 2011; Capps et al. 2005; Fry and Gonzales 2008). ELs who grow up in poverty thus face compounding risks, making them especially vulnerable to poor academic outcomes (Fry 2007; Wight, Chau, and Aratani 2010). And it is the case that in the United States, linguistic diversity and poverty are related; many U.S.–born children of immigrants and immigrant children are raised in poverty. The latest government statistics reveal that child poverty rates increased from 16.2 percent in 2000 to 21.6 percent in 2010 (Wight et al. 2010). With immigration rates also on the rise, children of immigrants now make up 24 percent of the school-age population. Strikingly, for example, approximately one in every three Latino children grows up in poverty, and many also enter school with limited proficiency in English (Lopez and Velasco 2011).

linguistic diversity is soon to be characteristic of all classrooms. Unless we further support educators to design instruction to match the demographics of today's students, as the EL population continues to grow and to grow up, so too will the number of students experiencing difficulties.

Defining *English Learner*

It is important for us to state that in this book, we use the term *English learner* to represent *all* students in our elementary school classrooms who come from households where a language other than English is the primary language spoken. Why? Well, the basis for distinguishing between limited versus full English proficiency is poorly defined and highly variable across different states and school districts. Most importantly, for the purposes of a conversation about instruction, many children from homes where English is not the primary language spoken and who are classified as fully English proficient on school entry or reclassified after receiving ESL services or even bilingual services still continue to need language supports. Many ELs with academic challenges in the later grades have been enrolled in U.S. schools since kindergarten, and they no longer have a formal designation justifying support services for language development. Recall that Ms. Parkin doesn't even really make distinctions between her students who are receiving language support services and those who have been reclassified. That is, for educators like Ms. Parkin, the need for language-based literacy support does not always line up with a student's language classification as determined by the district; instead, many ELs, including those who do not qualify to receive ESL services, require instruction that intentionally supports and promotes their continued language development. Consider, too, that what it means to be *proficient* changes as a function of the curriculum—a first grader's ability to meet the language demands of the curriculum is very different from the fourth grader's ability to do so. Being proficient at grade 1 is not the same as being proficient at grade 4—the game changes over time. A learner's language development therefore needs to keep pace with the changing language demands of the curriculum, and the classification system doesn't account for that. Finally, whether classified for support services or not, EL students entering U.S. schools must learn with enormous efficiency if they are to catch up with their monolingual English classmates. They typically score lower than monolingual students during the preschool years on assessments of vocabulary and oral language comprehension in English, and they are likely to have had fewer encounters with book reading and emergent literacy activities in any language (Hammer, Scarpino, and Davison 2011).

ENGLISH LEARNERS ARE NOT STRUGGLING THINKERS!

ELs vary in their English proficiency from beginning to intermediate to advanced levels. Limited proficiency in English should not be considered a sign of limited intelligence. Although this might seem obvious, in fact we know that oftentimes students' hesitancies to speak, errors, or accents are misinterpreted as signs of cognitive deficiencies (Cummins 2000). Yet ELs are just as capable as their peers who speak fluent English to engage in higher-level thinking. There is even a considerable amount of research evidence pointing to the cognitive benefits of bilingualism in both the short and long term (Bialystok, Craik, and Luk 2012). The issue is that as learners are still developing capacities to navigate more than one language, it might take them longer to process language, but processing time should not be confused with capability. Even when they seem fluent in oral English, they still might mentally translate to their first language when grappling with challenging content. Indeed, it is important to remember that second language acquisition is an *uneven* process (Bialystok 1991). ELs' relative proficiency in English can fluctuate for a number of reasons, not the least of which is topic at hand.

So, in this book we use the term *English learner* in the broadest sense, and we focus on the largest and fastest-growing population of ELs—those learners who are coming up through our educational system from the youngest ages.

Reading Development Among English Learners

For all readers, including our ELs, the process of reading development is both cumulative and componential (RAND Reading Study Group 2002). By *cumulative*, we mean that the process of reading development begins at birth and continues through adulthood. By developing skills and knowledge while accumulating reading experiences over time, a reader is able to keep pace with the changing demands of the context and the purpose for reading. This continual development creates a foundation for learning across all school subjects (RAND Reading Study

Group 2002; Shanahan and Shanahan 2008). After all, the school curriculum is conveyed largely through oral and written language. By *componential*, we mean a number of separate, but related, skills go into the process. Next, we spend some time discussing these skills to provide relevant information that helps us understand what it is we're learning about the reading process for ELs.

Distinguishing Between Code-Based and Meaning-Based Skills

When the parent of a first grader hears her child finally work through the pages of a text with ease, successfully reading *Hop on Pop* aloud, for example, there might be a sigh of relief and a feeling that the job of learning to read is done. But that sense of relief might be premature. "Reading" in grade 1 is not the same as "reading" in grade 8. With increasing grade levels, the demands of the texts children must read increase in difficulty, and yet text is the primary way that academic content is delivered to students, especially in middle school and high school (where all students are headed!). In fact, to be successful in all academic content areas, students need to be proficient readers. But what counts as proficient is always changing; to be a proficient reader throughout the years, a learner has to accumulate experiences at home, in her community, and in any formal educational setting that will build up her language and knowledge, to support her literacy development.

The question is—after daily instruction throughout the years, why do many students, including many ELs, struggle to comprehend texts? One major problem lies in whether children acquire both the skills and knowledge needed to read and understand complex texts. As illustrated in Figure 1.1, code-based competencies are those that allow students to master the mechanics of reading—for example, the ability to efficiently, even automatically, map letters onto their respective sounds in combinations, and thus read words. Meaning-based competencies, on the other hand, comprise the range of abilities and knowledge necessary for constructing our understanding of a text. They include the skills related to language development, such as oral language, vocabulary, and listening comprehension skills, as well as the foundational knowledge needed to access and apply a text's message. In fact, vocabulary knowledge, in particular, is so important for literacy development and achievement that the acquisition, use, and interpretation of words and phrases is represented in the College and Career Readiness anchor English language arts standards for: (1) reading literature, (2) reading information text, and (3) language (Common Core State Standards Initiative 2010). Also included in this broad group of skills are the cognitive strategies needed to facilitate meaning construction and learning (Alexander and Jetton 2000; Cain,

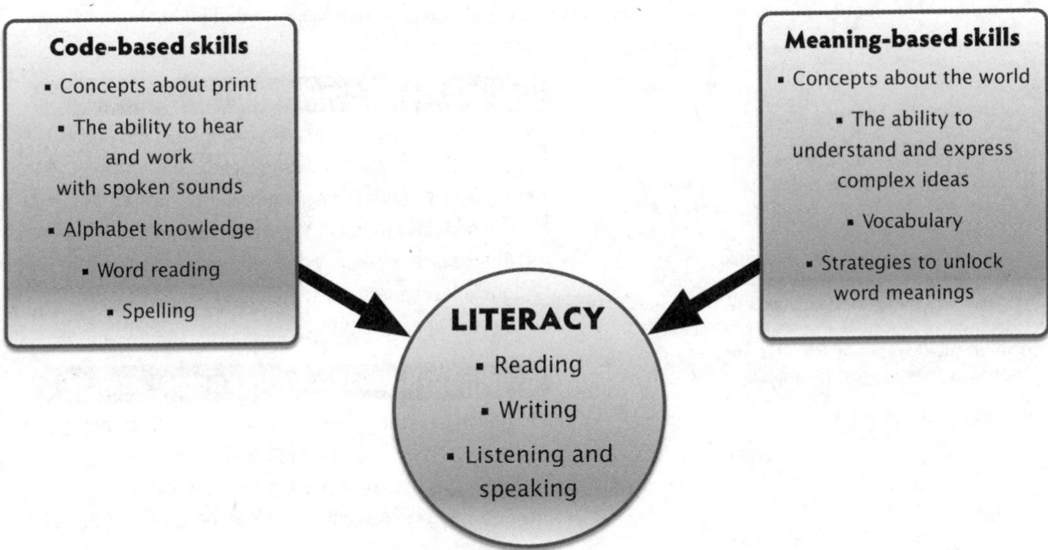
Code-based skills
▪ Concepts about print
▪ The ability to hear and work with spoken sounds
▪ Alphabet knowledge
▪ Word reading
▪ Spelling
Meaning-based skills
▪ Concepts about the world
▪ The ability to understand and express complex ideas
▪ Vocabulary
▪ Strategies to unlock word meanings
LITERACY
▪ Reading
▪ Writing
▪ Listening and speaking

Figure 1.1 Unpacking Literacy Competencies: Examples of Code- and Meaning-Based Skills

Oakhill, and Bryant 2004), such as those focused on comprehension monitoring and making inferences (Cain, Oakhill, and Bryant 2004) as well as those focused on unlocking the meanings of words using knowledge of meaningful word parts, context, and native language connections (Baker et al. 2014). Many researchers also include those skills associated with "prosodic" reading in this category: using appropriate expression, intonation, and phrasing as indicators of reading fluency, and therefore, comprehension supports (Kuhn et al. 2010).

The passage featured in Figure 1.2[1] and the corresponding diagram illustrate the distinction between code-based and meaning-based competencies in reading. To read even this short passage, the reader must be able to map sounds onto letters and recognize common spelling patterns, reading with enough automaticity and efficiency to then spend some time attending to the passage's meaning. If the reader takes too long, or the decoding experience is too laborious, the information from the beginning of the passage is no longer in memory. Although having these code-based competencies is necessary, it is not sufficient to support

---

1 Passage adapted from Good and Kaminski (2002).

High Speed Trains

A type of high-speed train was first introduced in Japan about forty years ago. The train was low to the ground, and its nose looked somewhat like the nose of a jet. These trains provided the first passenger service that moved at a speed of one hundred miles per hour. Today, similar Japanese trains are even faster, traveling at speeds of almost two hundred miles per hour. There are many reasons that high-speed trains are popular.

Code-Based Competencies

- Map sounds onto letters (e.g., /s/ /p/ /ee/ /d/) and blend these to form a word (speed).
- Recognize common spelling patterns, such as the "-igh" family found in the word "high."
- Read words accurately and efficiently—at the fifth-grade level, this means reading at least 115 words correctly per a minute.

Meaning-Based Competencies

- Understand the meanings of words in this context (e.g., "service" has 37 possible definitions!).
- Make meaning of text using relevant background knowledge (e.g., conceptual knowledge about trains and jets and travel).
- Use cognitive strategies (e.g., when reading the second sentence, if the child first pictures a human nose, he must be able to adjust when the comparison to a jet's nose is read).

Figure 1.2 What competencies does a reader need to make sense of this passage?

reading comprehension. Students also need meaning-based competencies, including understanding the meaning of the words in their contexts. In addition, the reader must have and deploy cognitive strategies aimed at monitoring meaning and repairing misunderstandings along the way. Without well-developed meaning-based competencies, having mastered the mechanics of reading becomes less and less valuable with time—for all readers, the core benefit of mastering the mechanics of print is to have the "mental space" to devote to making meaning from what is read.

Just like developing readers who are monolingual English speakers, research demonstrates that both code-based and meaning-related skills contribute to ELs' reading development, and ultimately, to their reading comprehension (Geva and Yaghoub Zadeh 2006; Gottardo and Mueller 2009; Mancilla-Martinez and Lesaux 2010; Proctor et al. 2005). Yet there are still important qualifications to this generally similar trend.

LITERACY DEVELOPMENT AND ACHIEVEMENT: BEYOND SKILLS AND KNOWLEDGE

The model of literacy that we use in this book (Figure 1.1) is useful for framing our discussion of research-based, high-quality instruction in classrooms serving ELs. But it is important to remind ourselves that many other interrelated competencies also influence literacy development. For example, all children's literacy competencies are inextricably linked with social and emotional skills, such that strength or weakness in one domain can facilitate or impede competence and achievement in the other (Raver, Garner, and Smith-Donald 2007; Zigler, Gilliam, and Jones 2006). In fact, Nonie's current research is focused on investigating how the domains of executive functioning and self-regulation are related to ELs' literacy development.

Beyond the social and emotional skills that influence learning and development there are physical and psychological factors that also come into play. When students, including ELs, come to schools hungry or much too tired, without corrective lenses or needed hearing aids, struggling with asthma, untreated health conditions, or without a sense of physical and psychological safety, their literacy development is compromised. And so, although the distinction between the "meaning-based skills" and "code-based skills" that go into literacy is particularly useful when making instructional decisions, even these overarching categories are limited. They are a good starting place for thinking about this broad concept we call "literacy," but there are many factors that come to bear on a child's developmental experience.

English Learners' Code-Based Skills Development

We know that phonological processing skills play a crucial role in children's word-reading development (National Reading Panel 2000), based on research primarily conducted with English-only learners. However, the evidence base now indicates that typically developing ELs perform comparably to their monolingual English-speaking peers on measures of phonological processing skills (Lesaux et al. 2006). Some research even suggests that ELs may outperform monolingual learners on measures of rapid naming speed and phonological awareness (August and Shanahan 2006; Geva and Yaghoub Zadeh 2006; Lesaux and Siegel 2003), but their working memory skills appear similar during the early stages of reading acquisition.

For ELs, like their monolingual English-speaking peers, these phonological processing skills (e.g., the emerging reader's ability to identify the four sounds in the word *speed*: /s/ /p/ /ee/ /d/) support the development of accurate and efficient word reading (August and Shanahan 2006; Gottardo and Mueller 2009; Lipka and Siegel 2007). For both groups, word reading draws on knowledge of letter–sound relationships and knowledge of high-frequency words (August and Shanahan 2006); with sufficient exposure to English reading instruction, both groups on average attain similar levels of word-reading accuracy and efficiency, whether assessed in elementary or middle school (August and Shanahan 2006; Betts et al. 2009; Geva and Yaghoub Zadeh 2006; Jean and Geva 2009; Lesaux, Crosson, et al. 2010; Lesaux, Rupp, and Siegel 2007; Mancilla-Martinez and Lesaux 2011). At the same time, we note that although some measures of word-reading fluency focus only on accuracy and efficiency and therefore we see comparable levels across ELs and their monolingual classmates, some research indicates that ELs may be more likely to struggle with bringing the right intonation and expression to text, thus compromising what many refer to as *fluent reading*; such assessment, however, demands the reading of connected text as opposed to word lists. Many suggest this difference may be due to the influence of oral language skills on this element of fluent reading (referred to as *prosody*; Al Otaiba et al. 2009; Geva and Yaghoub Zadeh 2006; Schilling et al. 2007). Together, these research findings indicate that when it comes to mastering the mechanics of reading, typically developing ELs, those not experiencing significant developmental issues and/or early impairments, readily reach skill levels similar to those of their monolingual English-speaking peers.

English Learners' Meaning-Based Skills Development

In contrast to what we've learned about the way in which ELs and their monolingual English-speaking peers tend to develop equivalent code-based skills, as a population, ELs are more likely to demonstrate underdeveloped meaning-based skills, such as their oral language, vocabulary, and listening comprehension skills (Betts et al. 2009; Geva and Yaghoub Zadeh 2006; Jean and Geva 2009; Mancilla-Martinez and Lesaux 2011). As a result, as shown in the data presented in Figure 1.3, there is often a disconnect between ELs' ability to read the words on the page and their comprehension of the words they read (Crosson and Lesaux 2010; Lesaux, Crosson et al. 2010; Lesaux et al. 2006; Mancilla-Martinez and Lesaux 2011). And ultimately, ELs' reading comprehension is more strongly related to, and more likely to be constrained by, meaning-related skills than by code-based skills (Lesaux et al. 2006; Lesaux, Crosson et al. 2010; Proctor et al. 2005; Swanson et al. 2008).

A longitudinal study that Nonie conducted with Jeannette Mancilla-Martinez illustrates this disconcerting trend: Many ELs are reading words but don't have sufficient word knowledge to support their reading comprehension (2011). This study, conducted with children born to Spanish-speaking immigrants and enrolled in Head Start programs in one of five locations in the Northeast, shows this code-meaning gap widening as participating children go from preschool through to the end of elementary school.

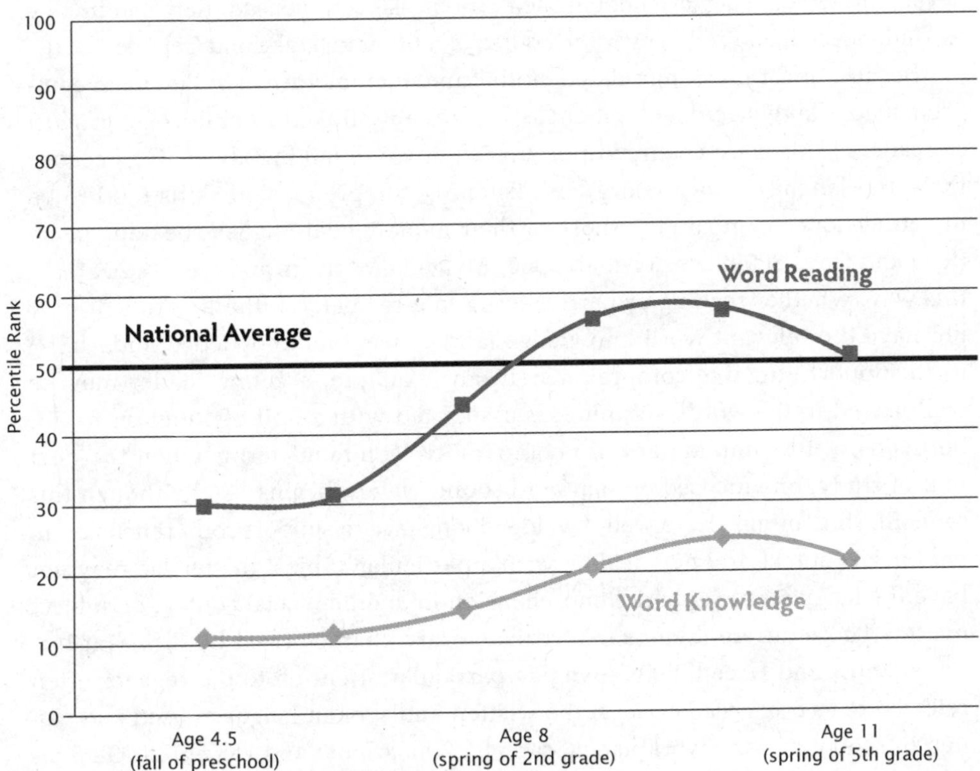

Figure 1.3 The Word Reading–Word Knowledge Gap

The Unique Challenges of Meaning-Based Skills

What is behind these differences in reading development between ELs and their monolingual English-speaking peers? The difference lies primarily in the nature of the skills themselves. Code-based skills are discrete and highly susceptible to instruction in a relatively brief time period (for a discussion see Paris 2005). For example, there are twenty-six letters in the English alphabet. Although they can appear in uppercase and lowercase forms, as well as in various fonts, the task of knowing letters is a constrained one—there are twenty-six! The limited universe of letters, and even their sound correspondences and combinations (forty-four sounds in total, represented by approximately 250 different spellings; Ball and Blachman 1991; Reed 2012), means that we teach for mastery. In contrast, meaning-related skills constitute a much larger problem space. For example, we know that the average reader needs a repertoire of an estimated fifty thousand words to draw on by the end of high school (Nagy and Anderson 1984). And, meaning-based skills are never "mastered." They are not checked off our lists, but instead, they continually expand, deepen, and refine over the course of a lifetime (Duke and Carlisle 2011).

Because most meaning-related skills fundamentally involve language comprehension, language development is inextricably linked to children's growth as readers. This is especially important when we're talking about ELs because their oral language, vocabulary, and listening comprehension skills tend to be underdeveloped compared to those of their monolingual English-speaking peers (Jean and Geva 2009; Lesaux et al. 2006; Mancilla-Martinez and Lesaux 2011). In this way, whether reading or participating in a read-aloud, the EL student may not have the relevant word knowledge (and conceptual knowledge underlying it) to support effective comprehension. For example, a young reader may be well versed in the words and phrases associated with a unit of study on neighborhoods, yet be unfamiliar with comparably "common" terms when the next unit of study, one focused on light and sound waves, begins. And although this same EL student may have well-developed language to support comprehension in one social context or when dealing with a particular subject matter, he may not have the language to support comprehension in another social context or subject matter. These different language "registers" are characterized by different features (Snow and Uccelli 2009); we pay particular attention to the register often referred to as *academic language*, the written and spoken language used and valued in school and the workplace (Scarcella 2003; Snow and Uccelli 2009). This register of language is central to all learners' literacy achievement and, therefore, academic success. Importantly, academic language stands in sharp contrast to everyday conversational language, even when the message communicated is similar. Imagine, for example, a sixth grader's description of a science experiment. Depending on the context and audience, the student's description of the experiment might be characterized by language features that are more typical of conversational or academic language. For instance, if the student was sharing the experience with her mother, she might begin the story by saying: "Mom, during science class today we did an activity and the craziest thing happened. Can I tell you about it?" On the other hand, if the same student were describing the event in a written paper for school, she would express herself differently, drawing on her academic language skills: "The data from the science experiment indicate unexpected results. The following report outlines the findings."

In both scenarios, the student's language choices are perfectly appropriate—the register used reflects the context and purpose for communication. Importantly, in the context of school (and for that matter, many professional settings), the texts students read are characterized by traits of the academic language register, and therefore, when it comes to school texts, students must have facility with the academic language register if they are to experience deep comprehension and learning.

In the next chapter, as part of a broader discussion about oral language, we zero in on the characteristics of academic language and the role it plays in ELs' literacy development and achievement, highlighting how instruction that fosters ELs' capacities with this register of the English language can open up a gateway for learning.

Closing Opportunity Gaps

The research reviewed in this chapter reminds us that it's not "reading" per se that impedes ELs' advanced literacy skill development; it's actually the language of print—in the newspaper, the textbook, the magazine article—that proves difficult and demands instructional emphasis. Our task, then, is to shift our model for teaching literacy to one that maintains strong code-based instruction but is even more intentional about building up the meaning-based competencies that go into literacy. And it can be done. In today's linguistically diverse classroom, research suggests that a classroom-wide, universal approach focused on building up academic vocabulary and conceptual knowledge holds huge promise. The past decade has seen a relative surge in classroom-based research focused on doing exactly this—providing ELs and their classroom peers with deep language- and content-based instruction, with a focus on teaching both specialized vocabulary and the specialized structures of language in academic speech and text. And so, in this book, we present what goes into this kind of knowledge-building approach to literacy instruction.

2

Understanding Oral Language for Literacy and the Special Case of Academic Language

Recounting how the seabird featured in their guided reading text catches and eats its prey, Javier explains, "The bird catches the fish underwater and eats it when he reaches the surface." Just as Ms. Parkin is about to nod in confirmation and move on, Javier continues, "The bird flies to land, or maybe in its nest or something, and then it eats." Although Javier's first explanation is nearly verbatim given the words on the page, his interpretation of "reaches the surface" is, well, wrong. Does he think surface is referring to land, rather than the top of the water? Ms. Parkin pauses. It's a relatively minor misunderstanding, she thinks, but she wonders how often this might be happening and what it means for Javier's reading comprehension. "Tell me more about that, Javier," Ms. Parkin probes, realizing she better dig deeper into this one.

The relationship between language and reading is not always an obvious one, especially when we think about how important it is that our learners be able to read the words on the page—with accuracy and automaticity. For that reason, we've mostly gone about literacy reform guided by the assumption that if we focus on the *act* of reading—putting the letters and sounds together to read words—then students will engage in deep comprehension. This turns out to be a flawed logic; it's true that we absolutely need to support students to develop strong word-reading skills, but thinking of these as the "gateway" to deep comprehension is where the logic breaks down. Why? Well, because of the role that language plays in connecting word reading to reading comprehension. This flawed logic has proven particularly problematic for academically vulnerable populations, including many of our English learners (ELs). Our task, then, is to redesign our model for teaching literacy with both word reading and language development in mind. In this chapter, building off our general discussion of literacy skills in Chapter 1, we focus on the language side of "reading"—how our learners' understanding of oral and written language is ultimately the linchpin for their reading comprehension. Because we're focused on ELs like Javier, we start by unpacking oral language, guided by the question: What, exactly, are the skills and competencies these learners need to acquire—and in a hurry? We then move to the special case of academic language, a hot topic within literacy reform today but one that can be elusive when we think about what is really meant by the term, and what it means for everyday teaching and learning.

What Is Oral Language?

Oral language is the system through which we use spoken words to express knowledge, ideas, and feelings. Developing ELs' oral language, then, means developing the skills and knowledge that go into listening and speaking—all of which have a strong relationship to reading comprehension and to writing. Discussed in more detail below, and as shown in Figure 2.1, broadly, oral language is made up of at least five key components (Moats 2010): phonological skills, pragmatics, syntax, morphological skills, and vocabulary (also referred to as *semantics*). All of these components of oral language are necessary to communicate and learn through conversation and spoken interaction, but there are important distinctions among them that have implications for literacy instruction.

A student's *phonological skills* are those that give her an awareness of the sounds of language, such as the sounds of syllables and rhymes (Armbruster, Lehr, and Osborne 2001). In addition to being important for oral language development, these skills play a foundational role in supporting word-reading development. In the early stages of learning how to read words, children are often encouraged to sound out the words. But before even being able to match the sounds to the letters, students need to be able to hear and understand the discrete sounds that make up language. As discussed in Chapter 1, phonological skills typically do not present lasting sources of difficulty for ELs; we know that under appropriate instructional circumstances, on average, ELs and their monolingual

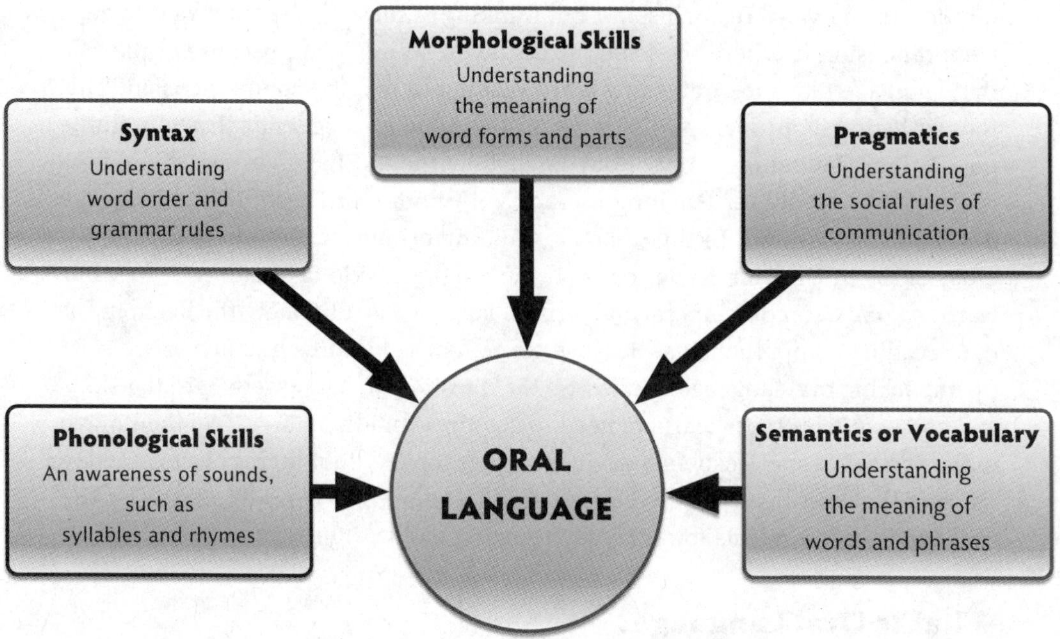

Figure 2.1 Components of Oral Language

English-speaking peers develop phonological skills at similar levels, and in both groups, these skills are mastered by the early elementary grades.

Students' skills in the domains of *syntax*, *morphology*, and *pragmatics* are central for putting together and taking apart the meaning of sentences and paragraphs, and for oral and written dialogue. *Syntax* refers to an understanding of word order and grammatical rules (Cain 2007; Nation and Snowling 2000). For example, consider the following two sentences:

Sentence #1: Relationships are preserved only with care and attention.
Sentence #2: Only with care and attention are relationships preserved.

In these cases, although the word orders are different, the sentences communicate the same message. In other cases, a slight change in word order alters a sentence's meaning. For example:

Sentence #1: The swimmer passed the canoe.
Sentence #2: The canoe passed the swimmer.

Morphology, discussed in more detail in Chapter 7, refers to the smallest meaningful parts from which words are created, including roots, suffixes, and prefixes (Carlisle 2000; Deacon and Kirby 2004). When a reader stumbles upon an unfamiliar word (e.g., *unpredictable*), an awareness of how a particular prefix or suffix (e.g., *un-* and *-able*) might change the meaning of a word or how two words with the same root may relate in meaning to each other (e.g., *predict*, *predictable*, *unpredictable*) supports her ability to infer the unfamiliar word's meaning. In fact, for both ELs and monolingual English speakers, there is a reciprocal relationship between morphological awareness and reading comprehension, and the strength of that relationship increases throughout elementary school (Carlisle 2000; Deacon and Kirby 2004; Goodwin et al. 2013; Kieffer, Biancarosa, and Mancilla-Martinez 2013; Nagy, Berninger, and Abbott 2006).

Pragmatics refers to an understanding of the social rules of communication (Snow and Uccelli 2009). So, for example, pragmatics involve how we talk when we have a particular purpose (e.g., persuading someone versus appeasing someone), how we communicate when we're engaging with a particular audience (e.g., a family member versus an employer), and what we say when we find ourselves in a particular context (e.g., engaging in a casual conversation versus delivering a public speech). These often implicit social rules of communication differ across content areas or even text genres. Pragmatics play a role in reading comprehension because much of making meaning from text depends upon having the right ideas about the norms and conventions for interacting with others—to understand feelings, reactions, and dilemmas among characters or populations,

UNEVEN DEVELOPMENT: ANYTHING BUT UNUSUAL

As we touched upon in Chapter 1, second language acquisition is by nature an uneven developmental process (Bialystok 1991). Therefore, ELs' facility with the different components of oral language typically varies at any given time point, and it is common for ELs to be stronger in some dimensions of language than others (Solano-Flores 2006). For instance, some ELs might have relatively strong vocabulary knowledge but struggle with grammar (or vice versa).

for example, and even to make inferences and predictions. The reader has to be part of the social world of the text for effective comprehension.

Finally, having the words to engage in dialogue—the *vocabulary knowledge*—is also a key part of oral language, not to mention comprehending and communicating using print (Beck, McKeown, and Kucan 2013; Ouellette 2006). Vocabulary knowledge, also referred to as *semantic* knowledge, involves understanding the meanings of words and phrases (aka *receptive vocabulary*) and using those words and phrases to communicate effectively (aka *expressive vocabulary*). Notably, vocabulary knowledge exists in degrees, such that any learner has a particular "level" of knowledge of any given word (Beck, McKeown, and Kucan 2013). This begins with the word sounding familiar and moves toward the ability to use the word flexibly, even metaphorically, when speaking and writing. Vocabulary knowledge must be fostered from early childhood through adolescence. Discussed in more detail in Chapter 6, deep vocabulary knowledge is often a source of difficulty for ELs, hindering their literacy development (August and Shanahan 2006).

All told, whether we're interpreting speech or print, we draw on these components of oral language to make meaning. Each component has a role to play in the comprehension process and all are amenable to instruction (see Figure 2.2 for

Phonological Skills: Precursors to Early Word Reading	**Syntax, Morphological Skills, and Pragmatics: The Glue of Oral Language**	**Semantics/Vocabulary: A Cornerstone of Oral Language**
▪ Enable a listener to differentiate the words in a stream of spoken language ▪ Unlike the other components of oral language, these skills are discrete and typically mastered by first grade ▪ Require limited instruction, pre-K through early elementary school	▪ Enable learners to make sense of what they hear and to communicate ideas in ways that make sense to others ▪ Develop from infancy through adulthood ▪ Require sustained instruction, pre-K–12	▪ Represents a learner's conceptual knowledge about the world. After all, you can't separate big ideas from the words that represent them! ▪ Develops from infancy through adulthood ▪ Requires sustained instruction, pre-K–12

Figure 2.2 What makes the components of oral language distinct?

a summary). When we look carefully at the language demands of reading comprehension, especially through the eyes of our large and fast-growing population of ELs, it becomes very clear that if students do not understand the language used and the concepts the language describes, "reading" the printed page will not result in comprehension or learning. Schools have done a good job teaching many of our ELs and their classmates the basic skills necessary to be proficient readers in the early grades, decoding and comprehending the conversational language that conveys ideas and topics in beginner books. So that's oral language. But what about *academic language*? Many are using the term, but it's not always clear what exactly is meant.

The Special Case of Academic Language

As you might recall, oral language involves the skills and knowledge that go into listening and speaking; it is the system through which we use and interpret spoken words that express knowledge, ideas, and feelings. Oral language comprises multiple elements, including vocabulary, syntax, and morphology. When we use language, knitting together words and phrases to communicate our thoughts, each element of language can take on fewer or more of the characteristics that are typical of academic text and talk. In that sense, as defined here, oral language is the umbrella, and academic language is one register of oral language. By *register*, we mean language used for a particular purpose or in a particular social setting that is characterized by a particular constellation of traits (Schleppegrell 2001).

It's also important to remind ourselves that academic language can be oral *or* written. In fact, written academic language is more likely to have even more of the traits we describe as "academic" than oral academic language. And so, for many ELs, comprehending and writing academic language can pose a particular challenge.

Unpacking Academic Language

For both young children and adolescents, academic success means having academic language—an essential tool for reading, writing, and critical thinking. Put plainly, academic language is the language used and valued for communicative purposes in school, higher education, and many professional settings; it is the language of school texts, assessments, and of influence (Scarcella 2003; Nagy and Townsend 2012). Although aspects of academic language vary among the content areas (even among text genres), here we focus on those characteristics of academic language that are considered common across the content areas, from the science textbook to the historical essay.

A number of characteristics together make language *academic*. In Figure 2.3, taking the elements of oral language described previously, we highlight some of the ways that these elements can be characterized by more academic traits. These characteristics of academic language are often described as existing on one end of a continuum, with everyday, social, conversational language at the other extreme (Snow 2010). In that sense, while still drawing upon the language skills and competencies we described above, academic language represents a different way of *using* language than the way we use it in the everyday setting. That is, the academic register differs from the register we use for social, conversational language; in the everyday register, as compared to the academic register, we use

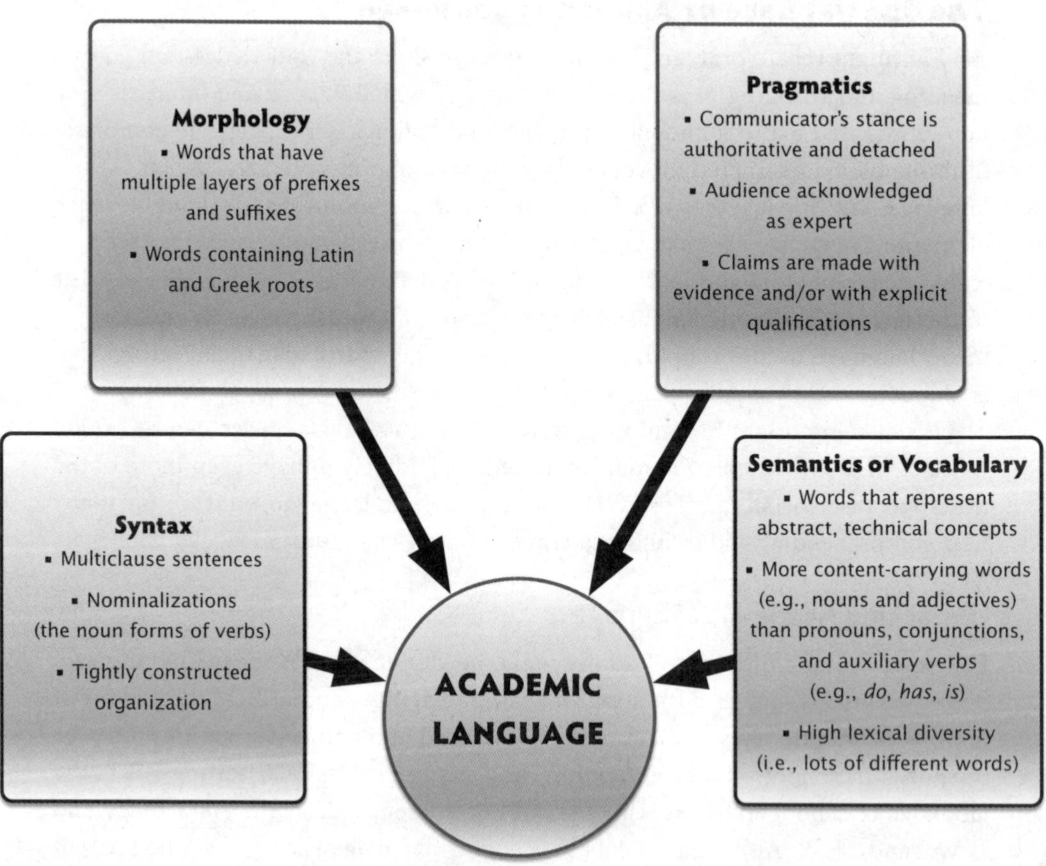

Figure 2.3 What makes language academic?

fewer words, words that tend to be high frequency in nature, and we speak in shorter sentences. We also repeat ourselves more often to ensure understanding, and we more often talk about the here and the now. For example, in everyday language, we might call (or text) a family member with the message:

I'll be home in a bit—less than an hour. See you then.

In the example above, the words are all high frequency (e.g., *home, see*), including a high proportion of pronouns (e.g., *I, you*) and auxiliary verbs (e.g., *be*); the sentences are brief (i.e., 3–10 words each); and the stance is relatively informal and personal. Using the academic register, however, we could communicate the same message differently, explaining:

In the absence of further delay, homecoming, and a subsequent family convening, will occur within the hour.

Here, higher-frequency words (e.g., *will, family, hour*) are strung together with many more rare (e.g., *homecoming*) and academic (e.g., *subsequent, convening*) terms, all of which carry content necessary to understanding the message; the sentence is relatively long (seventeen words), and contains multiple clauses. The message is communicated with an authoritative tone and includes a specific caveat, warning that the claim will only be true "in the absence of further delay." As unrealistic as the second message might be in the context of calling home with an ETA, it is only unlikely because this more personal, informal context calls for a similarly casual register of language.

Although we said earlier that academic language is the "language of school texts," leveled readers often represent exceptions to this rule and are another example of everyday language used in the classroom. Leveled readers are written for learners who are still developing their code-based reading skills and therefore have relatively fewer features of academic language when compared to trade books used as read-alouds in the classroom, geared toward students' listening comprehension levels. Take, for example, the excerpt from the book *Rain Forest* (considered a level L on the Fountas and Pinnell Text Level Gradient), featured in Figure 2.4. If you look closely at the language used in this leveled reader, you'll find that rain forests are described much more conversationally when compared to the way rain forests are described in the book *Adaptations*—a trade book about animal adaptations in various habitats, most appropriate for reading aloud in grades 3–5. Figure 2.5 outlines some of these differences. You can likely find even more. Again, it's not that one text is more valuable than the other—it's that they serve very different, important purposes. But make no mistake, all of our ELs

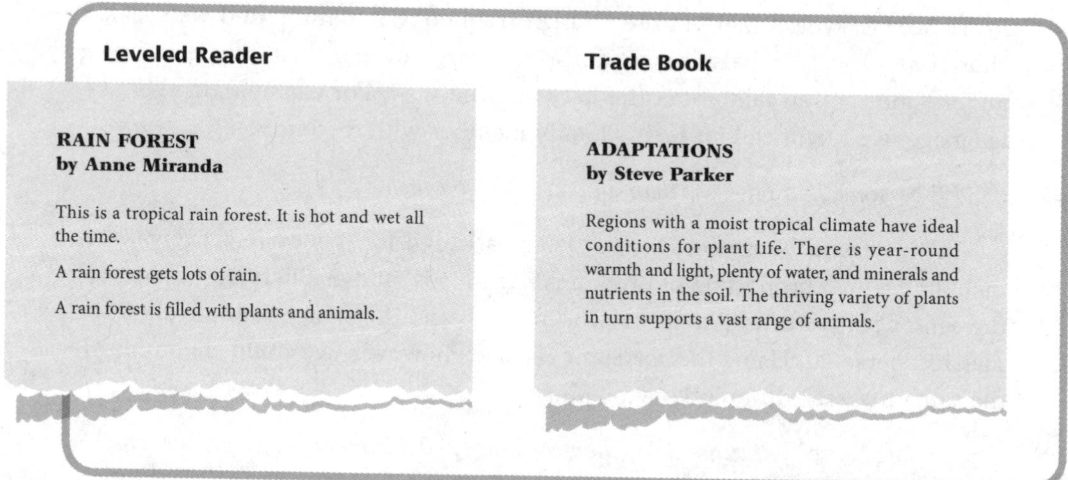

Leveled Reader

RAIN FOREST
by Anne Miranda

This is a tropical rain forest. It is hot and wet all the time.

A rain forest gets lots of rain.

A rain forest is filled with plants and animals.

Trade Book

ADAPTATIONS
by Steve Parker

Regions with a moist tropical climate have ideal conditions for plant life. There is year-round warmth and light, plenty of water, and minerals and nutrients in the soil. The thriving variety of plants in turn supports a vast range of animals.

Figure 2.4 How do the language demands differ in various kinds of school texts?

	Leveled Reader: ***Rain Forest*** **by Anne Miranda**	**Trade Book:** ***Adaptations*** **by Steve Parker**
Semantics or Vocabulary	High-frequency words and phrases: ▪ *all the time* ▪ *hot* ▪ *filled with plants and animals*	Words and phrases more commonly used in academic texts: ▪ *year-round* ▪ *warmth and light* ▪ *ideal conditions for plant life; supports a vast range of animals*
Syntax	Nouns and noun phrases at the beginning of sentences concretely state the subject. ▪ The noun phrase *A rain forest* begins two of the sentences in this passage. This noun phrase represents a concrete concept: The lush, misty forest featured in the photograph on the page.	Noun phrases at the beginning of many sentences include densely packed information, often representing complex concepts explained in the preceding text. ▪ To fully comprehend the phrase *The thriving variety of plants*, the reader needs to remember that rain forests have ideal conditions for plant life and then readers have to make the cognitive leap to understanding that these conditions result in an environment where lots of different plants thrive. (Not to mention, the reader has to know the meaning of *thriving* and *variety* to even begin to comprehend this noun phrase.)

Figure 2.5 Similar Content, Different Language Features

need to be able to comprehend, and ultimately generate, texts that are similar to the trade book example.

When we support students' development of academic language, we are helping them to add to their linguistic funds of knowledge so that they can comprehend and generate the language used in academic and professional settings. As the previous examples illustrate, developing ELs' academic language skills means that they will have the ability to discuss events in a register appropriate for family talk *and* be able to write about those events using descriptions that feature academic words, syntax, and tone; it means that they will be able to read and comprehend the language of leveled readers *and* be able to comprehend and talk about grade-level texts, including trade books.

The Connection Between Academic Language and Reading Comprehension

What we're seeing in today's classrooms, especially through the window that ELs give us into the relationship between language and reading, is that even when conversational English is acquired with relative ease and we might consider an individual EL to be proficient, the need to comprehend and produce academic language for academic success may still present a significant challenge (Nagy and Townsend 2012). And as discussed in Chapter 1 and here, it's important to bear in mind that many ELs acquire early word reading skills on par with their peers, and many of them are well past the "survival English" stage—they are conversant and comfortable speaking English and therefore have acquired the oral language skills and competencies needed to get there. This is especially the case after many years in American schools.

Still, with increasing grade levels, in part due to instructional opportunities and the everyday language used in our classrooms, the language of print becomes beyond their reach; it is even less conversational and much more academic, making the texts far more difficult to comprehend. Students' language use (and therefore knowledge) isn't always sufficiently sophisticated for the academic setting—and the same goes for their written language development; the language that many ELs are using to produce written products is not academic or technical enough to meet today's standards for what it means to be literate. And we all know of many of our ELs' classmates from English-speaking households who are in the same situation. This is especially the case in large, urban districts where many students, ELs and monolingual English speakers, experience a language of the home and community that is different from the academic language used in our texts, assessments, postsecondary classrooms, and workplaces. The academic language of print is, therefore, at once, a gatekeeper and a gateway. When academic language is largely inaccessible, so too is the school curriculum; accessing the language, however, means having the opportunity to learn academic concepts and generate ideas and questions that contribute to academic conversations and ultimately leads to school achievement.

It is especially important to mention that our students' difficulties in this domain do not necessarily signal a learning difficulty. Why? Well, first, ELs' rates of growth in language development surpass the rates of their peers (Kieffer 2008, 2010; Mancilla-Martinez and Lesaux 2011). That is, while they may be learning more words than their peers throughout the school years, many of their monolingual English-speaking classmates started out with more words. So, although many ELs might not "catch up" to their monolingual English-speaking peers over time, we know that for the vast majority this is not an "ability to learn" problem. Second, despite their strong relationship with academic achievement, we know that very little instructional time in elementary and secondary school focuses on developing academic language skills (Gilbert and Graham 2010; Kiuhara, Graham, and Hawken 2009; Lesaux, Kieffer et al. 2010; Scott, Jamieson-Noel, and Asselin 2003). If we don't give our learners explicit, intensive, and sustained opportunities to develop academic language, then we can't make claims about their ability to learn them. So let's turn to a more in-depth discussion of academic language.

Academic Language in Action

Now, let's go ahead and take a few examples of the academic language our learners need for success. Let's start with a read-aloud scenario in the kindergarten classroom down the hall from Ms. Parkin's room, then let's return to Ms. Parkin's room and revisit the case of Javier and his classmates reading the text about the seabird, and then, finally, let's move down the hall from Ms. Parkin's classroom, where the sixth graders are working on a debate project focused on economic principles and professional athletes' salaries.

Kindergarten

Ms. Strong, the kindergarten teacher, has just finished morning meeting, and her students are ready for today's read-aloud. The book *A House for Hermit Crab* by Eric Carle is connected to what they've been studying for more than a week now—life in the sea. Ms. Strong moves through the pages, stopping to pause along the way and ask some key questions. Upon reflection, she's

A HOUSE FOR HERMIT CRAB
by Eric Carle

In April, Hermit Crab passed a flock of starfish moving slowly along the sea floor.

"How handsome you are!" said Hermit Crab.

"Would one of you be willing to decorate my house?"

"I would," signaled a little sea star.

Carefully, Hermit Crab picked it up with his claw and put it on his house.

Semantics or Vocabulary

- Understand the meaning of words in this context (e.g., *pass* has 85 possible definition and is likely used differently here than in the classroom, i.e., "pass the crayons")
- Understand Hermit Crab is doing the action—*passing*—and the flock of starfish is receiving the action, being *passed*

Morphological Skills

- Understand that the suffix *-ly* changes the words *slow* and *careful* from action words to words that describe actions

Pragmatics

- Understand that read-aloud time is a time to listen and think about the story; spoken responses are appropriate when the teacher asks a question

Phonological Skills

- "Hear" the four different words that make up the phrase, *How handsome you are*

Figure 2.6 What language competencies do young learners need to make sense of this read-aloud?

surprised by how little some of her students seemed to grasp what, exactly, was happening in the interactions between the hermit crab and the various sea creatures. Many of her students seemed to understand the friendly tenor of these interactions and the general idea that the hermit crab was decorating his shell, but the characteristics of each creature and the ways in which these characteristics benefited the growing community living on and in the shell didn't seem as transparent as she thought.

In fact, the written language of many storybooks can present challenges for the listener that are unique from those posed by everyday, conversational language. Even in the earliest grades, relatively sophisticated language skills are required for deep comprehension of many of our favorite read-alouds. Although more concentrated in informational texts, narrative texts like *A House for Hermit Crab* include language features that are typical of academic language.

Grade 3

Now, let's return to Ms. Parkin's classroom from the opening of this chapter, with Javier struggling to make meaning from the text, but not because he isn't reading the words on the page with automaticity and fluency. As you might recall, the seabird in the text dives into the water, catching fish while beneath the water's surface. When the bird "reaches the surface" of the water, it swallows the fish. What's tripping Javier up is the language of the text, the notion of "reaching the surface." This is, after all, an abstract idea conveyed with academic vocabulary. Both *reach* and *surface* are words with multiple meanings and uses. They are used relatively frequently—we may not initially think they require particular explanation in a third-grade classroom—but as used in this scenario, they present a linguistic challenge. And in this case, Javier's interpretation of the text's language is changing the meaning for him. He's actively engaged with the text, drawing meaning and making inferences where he can—but his inference leads him astray, toward an unintended meaning.

Grade 6

Finally, let's consider a different scenario. Rafael, one of Ms. Parkin's former students, is now in sixth grade and preparing for a class debate about whether or not professional athletes deserve their high salaries. It is the culminating project after an economics unit during which he and his classmates read and discussed texts focused on resources, income, and market value. The topic of this debate is right up Rafael's alley: Unless required to do otherwise, he exclusively reads sports magazines. He and his friends regularly talk about the salaries of their favorite players, and on more than one occasion they have collectively imagined their own potential as professional athletes and all they could do with their millions. In preparation for this debate, he works with his peers to organize their arguments—writing down their main points, rationale, and evidence. They practice expressing their points of view orally and generate rebuttals in anticipation of the other groups' opposing claims. Rafael is integrating his knowledge of professional sports with his developing understanding of economics, and language is the medium through which these connections are made. Preparing for and engaging in this debate is pushing Rafael to stretch his language competencies. The oral and written language skills he needs to be able to engage in this classroom project involve more abstract and specialized vocabulary, more complex sentence structures, and more tightly constructed arguments (with substantive evidence) than he needs to carry out his friendly banter about sports players and athletic aspirations.

In Rafael's classroom, much like the third graders in Ms. Parkin's room and the kindergartners in Ms. Strong's class, learning experiences are anchored in texts featuring rich content. The language of text becomes increasingly sophisticated as we move up the grades, but all texts are marked by the academic register: therefore, if students are to benefit from the learning experiences school activities and texts afford, and if students are to be able to engage with academic language as Rafael does, our classroom talk and instruction must provide the appropriate scaffolds to do so.

Implications for the Design of Literacy Instruction

Our skilled readers and writers have well-developed academic language skills—an understanding of the words, phrases, and sentences that is needed to unpack and produce text filled with big ideas and complex concepts, for academic purposes. For many ELs, developing academic language skills has proven challenging. These trends notwithstanding, it's more important to point out that the comprehension and production of this language register presents a challenge *not* because it cannot be taught and learned. In fact, we're certain it can be taught and learned. But in most classrooms we are not teaching the academic register—consequently, many students have limited exposure to it and minimal experiences using it (Scarcella 2003; Schleppegrell 2001). And our ELs depend upon this instruction for their academic success.

Therefore, from our preschool classrooms, taking *A House for Hermit Crab* as a key example, through to our high school content area classes, where topics like chemical processes, historical ambiguities, and biodiversity furnish school texts, there are important ways that we can and must support all students, especially our growing population of ELs, to develop the skills they need for academic success. The only way to do this is to spend more time providing intentional, intensive support in developing their oral and written language skills—building up their specialized knowledge about language and the world.

In the remaining chapters of this book, we support your shift to an instructional model that focuses much more explicitly on the relationship between language and reading—a relationship that is not always an obvious one.

The Knowledge-Building Classroom

Deep, Process-Oriented, and Interactive Learning

Instructional Principles for the Knowledge-Building Classroom

"Whoa, it turned into a snake!" Javier, a third grader, is amazed as Ms. Parkin reads aloud a section of *Butterflies and Moths*, by Nic Bishop (featured in Figure 3.1). As Ms. Parkin holds up the book's larger-than-life photograph, allowing her students to view the caterpillar as it attempts to deceive its predator, Javier's expression is mirrored by many of his peers.

When scared, this rain forest caterpillar twists its body around and puffs up its front end to look like a poisonous snake. It even waves its body like a snake. But look closely and you will see that its snake eyes are not real. They are black-and-white markings normally hidden underneath the caterpillar.

Bishop 2009, 17

Figure 3.1 Caption Beside Photo in *Butterflies and Moths* by Nic Bishop

Ms. Parkin and her students are studying the ways that animals survive in their environments and she is using this rich, engaging text as a platform for learning. "It is extraordinary," Ms. Parkin replies. "In this photograph, this creature looks more like a snake than a caterpillar—I can hardly recognize it! Let's read the caption beside the photograph to see why this caterpillar disguises itself as a snake. Then, we'll do our 'think-pair-share' routine to talk through our ideas." After Ms. Parkin reads the caption, she reminds her third graders of the question they will discuss.

"Hmm. Why does this rain forest caterpillar disguise itself, mimicking a snake? What do you think?" She then quickly reviews the classroom's think-pair-share procedure and provides students with the chance to do the first step in this routine: think through their responses.

Ms. Parkin watches as Javier's head turns toward the academic word wall, looking for a reminder of the definition of *disguise*. Her class has encountered and used this word before, but it was in the context of an instructional unit about overcoming obstacles, in which they read a text featuring Harriet Tubman, who would disguise herself and her passengers on the Underground Railroad. Now, the topic has shifted from social awareness and history to the life sciences; she purposefully weaves in words and concepts from one unit to the next.

After her students have had adequate thinking time, she asks them to turn and discuss their thoughts with a partner. When Javier turns away from the word wall and toward his think-pair-share partner, Camilla, Ms. Parkin keeps her eye on him. She notices that the pair has really internalized the routine, and when the class comes back together, Ms. Parkin asks Javier and Camilla to share their discussion. After a pause, Javier begins: "Um, that caterpillar is a disguise. It looks like a snake so nothing will eat it." As Javier goes on, and Camilla adds to the conversation, Ms. Parkin hears several things that will influence her teaching—the students have a deepening understanding of how animals' abilities to camouflage themselves benefit their survival, but they need additional learning opportunities to build on this knowledge of the concept of disguise. She knows that as the unit and the year progress, they will have plenty of chances to do just that.

What do instructional approaches that effectively support English learners' (ELs) literacy development have in common? They focus on cultivating knowledge, and, in so doing, they build strong oral and written language skills. A knowledge-building approach to literacy instruction brings the world to students in meaningful ways, supporting them to develop the foundation they need to access and generate a range of texts now and as they grow up.

In light of what goes into literacy success—as we discussed in Chapter 1—the crucial role of knowledge building in effective literacy instruction shouldn't come as a surprise. After all, big ideas and complex questions cannot be separated from the language used to represent them. For example, a reader's comprehension of a story depends greatly upon the knowledge and language she brings to the experience. And a writer's ability to communicate his ideas and reach his audience depends greatly upon the knowledge and language he has to draw on.

In many classrooms and schools, the kind of approach we are describing here—the one Ms. Parkin takes—is going to mean a big shift, but a worthwhile one, especially for our ELs. In the sections that follow, we outline three principles that should guide instructional planning and serve as anchors for daily practice:

1. Go for depth of learning.
2. Focus on the learning process.
3. Make learning interactive.

These principles support the shift to knowledge-building literacy instruction. You'll notice that each one can and should be put to use in the service of the others. They are interrelated—applying them in concert with one another in your classroom creates powerful learning and teaching opportunities.

Principle #1: Go for depth of learning.

Instruction that effectively cultivates knowledge—and therefore supports advanced literacy development—focuses on the *depth of learning*. Why? Because knowledge exists in degrees; for any given subject, concept, or word, a learner has a particular level (or degree, as noted) of understanding. When we engage in knowledge-building literacy instruction—placing a concept, word, or theme at the center of our instructional design—that level of understanding deepens, setting ELs up to comprehend, discuss, and compose sophisticated texts.

Let's think about how depth of knowledge influences what it means to really *know* a word, for example. Figure 3.2 illustrates one way of thinking about our degrees of word knowledge, moving from shallow to deep understanding. This continuum has been discussed by several researchers over the last several decades, including Dale (1965); Beck, McKeown, and Omanson (1987); Beck, McKeown, and Kucan (2013); and Graves, August, and Mancilla-Martinez (2013).

So, what might this mean for a student and his knowledge of a particular word? Let's take the example of the word *substitute*. A student with shallow knowledge of the word might know that a *substitute* is someone who fills in for her absent teacher, but she is unable to use that word flexibly, even metaphorically, when speaking and writing because she doesn't have the underlying concept. She might be perplexed when the instructions in the science experiment explain, "You can substitute sand for the soil." When students lack deep understanding of multiple meanings, and different word forms like *substitution*, they are more likely to experience specific breakdowns in literacy activities, whether reading, writing, listening, or speaking.

To be sure (and let's spread the word on this!), it's not that our ELs don't have language—as we know, many are well beyond the beginning stages of

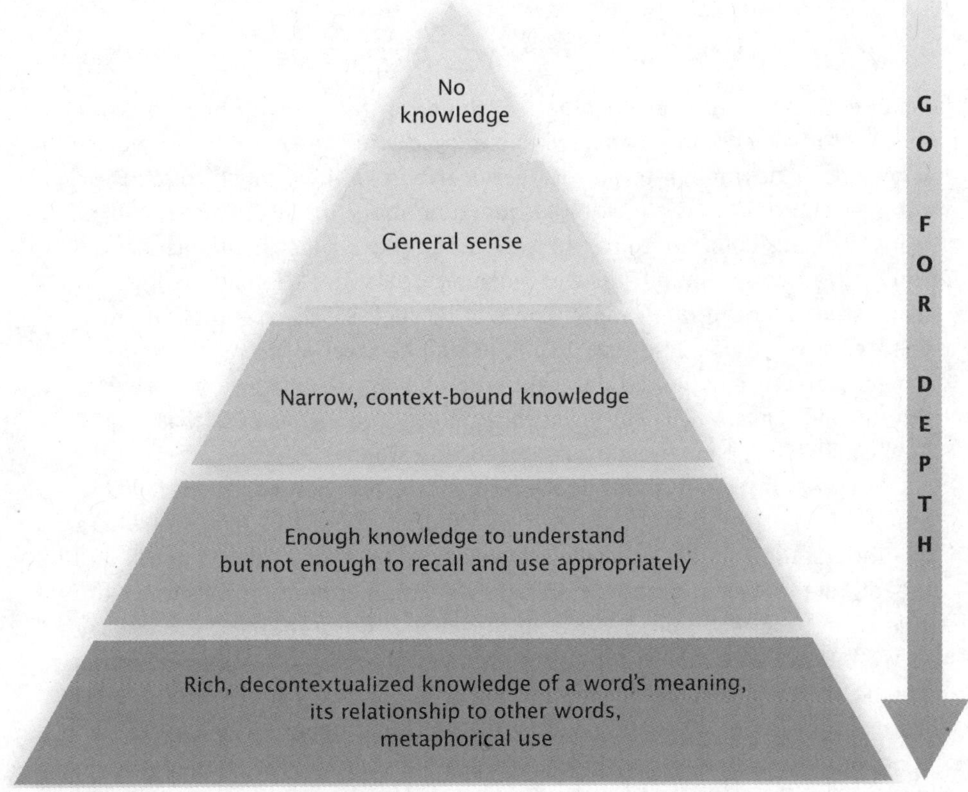

(Adapted from Beck, McKeown, and Kucan 2013, 11)

Figure 3.2 What does it mean to know a word?

English proficiency (for a discussion, see Lesaux 2012). But when it comes to the words and concepts that are most critical for long-term academic success (e.g., academic words like *substitute*), many ELs are operating somewhere between very shallow and deep knowledge (e.g., between levels 2 and 4 in the diagram). That is, they have *some* knowledge of many words and concepts—and often, that knowledge is deep enough to engage in day-to-day conversations, or get the gist of a story (August and Shanahan 2006; Harris and Lesaux 2014). But many ELs often require even deeper understanding of academic words and concepts to support reading comprehension or to comfortably and effectively enter academic conversations.

MAKING SENSE OF DEPTH VS. BREADTH

Many educators (and researchers) continue to grapple with how to strike the right instructional balance when charged with developing vocabulary knowledge—how much to go for deep learning vs. how much to focus on wide teaching. This is the age-old question about breadth vs. depth. For many, it seems counterintuitive to lean more toward a less-is-more approach when faced with a laundry list of learning goals and the knowledge that many students need *many* more words to be successful. To complicate matters, research studies find that distinguishing between depth and breadth is a measurement puzzle and different studies point us in varying directions (Kieffer and Lesaux 2012b; Pearson, Hiebert, and Kamil 2007; Nagy and Townsend 2012; Tannenbaum, Torgesen, and Wagner 2006).

But what if it's not about depth *or* breadth, but instead, about facilitating one to get to the other? What if we thought about this in a way where we understand that we can take advantage of just how related depth and breadth are? We're finding that, in fact, we can. By going for depth, we are able to in part accomplish the goal of developing breadth of vocabulary as well. How? Well, going for depth requires studying a number of words around the target word—meaning that for every one target word, several words are learned. When we take the time to build deep vocabulary knowledge, our instruction also includes a focus on metacognitive strategies (e.g., monitoring for meaning, problem solving, information seeking)—a focus that is much less compatible with covering many topics quickly. Heightened metacognition is requisite for taking full advantage of all of the less-intensive learning opportunities students encounter—such as the relatively brief or independent exposure to new ideas and concepts as part of a read-aloud or while reading independently. Therefore, over time, building up a deep understanding of a small(er) set of topics and words, in part done through instruction in metacognitive skills, results in an increased capacity to build breadth of knowledge.

What does this look like in Ms. Parkin's classroom?

To go for depth of learning, Ms. Parkin has shifted to a "less-is-more" approach. At first, she had some reservations about going for depth over breadth. After all, she is all too aware that the majority of her ELs are racing the clock and the calendar to "catch up." Part of her felt like she should be exposing her students to *as much* material as possible.

Now, her experience is confirming that it's a fine balance. She knows that ELs need to learn as much as possible, but she is also realizing that exposure and teaching for deep learning are not the same thing. When she goes for exposure—bringing many different ideas and skills to her students—she finds that it is often at the expense of deep learning. Exposure might help ELs in her classroom begin to make sense of the world, but it doesn't necessarily deepen their own knowledge base nor develop their language. And she is also cognizant that she can't possibly teach her students *all* of the content and concepts that are out there in the world and that they might need.

For these reasons, Ms. Parkin is thoughtful and purposeful when she designs instruction. She ensures that topics and target words are high impact for her students' academic achievement: meaty concepts that lend themselves to examination (e.g., adaptation for survival or overcoming obstacles); abstract words that are relevant to the topic at hand but also very useful for learning and talking across the curriculum (e.g., *disguise, survive, environment*); and multifaceted questions, without easy, clear-cut answers, that prompt thoughtful and extended discussions (e.g., Why do certain behaviors or physical adaptations benefit an organism's survival?).

SPOTLIGHT ON COLLEGE AND CAREER READINESS ENGLISH LANGUAGE ARTS STANDARDS AND THE ROLE OF DEEP LEARNING

We said it once, and we'll say it again: Knowledge-building classrooms do not "cover" standards—they go for depth of learning and accomplish standards along the way. Not only do today's new College and Career Readiness Standards, including the Common Core State Standards (CCSS), lend

— continues —

— continued —

themselves to instruction that goes for depth of learning, but these new standards demand it (Common Core State Standards Initiative 2010). In fact, consider, for example, Reading Anchor Standard 8 of the CCSS: Students will be able to evaluate the argument and specific claims in a text. Learning to evaluate a text sufficiently and successfully, as Standard 8 requires, means coming back to it several times, studying it, and discussing the multifaceted evidence and potential biases it features. Likewise, students will not comprehend and use accurately a range of general academic and domain-specific words and phrases (Language Anchor Standard 6) if we do not study these words—and the concepts they represent—with a focus on how words work and relate to each other, providing students with opportunities to grapple with degrees of meaning, depending on context and use. And when it comes to developing the content knowledge it takes to comprehend increasingly complex texts, the CCSS provides explicit guidance. In the section titled, "Staying on Topic Within a Grade and Across Grades," the importance of reading and discussing multiple texts that relate to a single topic over a sustained period is underscored, with the goal of providing opportunities for students to build depth of understanding (CCSS Initiative 2010, 33).

In so doing, Ms. Parkin does not "cover" standards, nor simply scratch the surface of any given topic, and move on. Instead, her instruction focuses on the study of concepts, words, and questions from several angles, using multiple methods, over an extended period of time. Make no mistake, she still sometimes has the feeling that she's "doing less." She supposes that, in some ways, she is. But it is in the kind of literacy environment she is cultivating that learning opportunities really add up, and her ELs' language and knowledge accumulate.

Principle #2: Focus on the learning process.

Our second principle of knowledge-building literacy instruction focuses on process. Knowledge-building literacy instruction is necessarily *process-oriented*. Here, our orientation toward the learning process has to do with the ways in which knowledge develops. As you might recall from Chapter 1, a defining characteristic of code-based literacy skills is that they are discrete. Readers can master these skills, so our teaching can have a very specific and clear end goal and we can assess to determine mastery. For example, there are twenty-six letters in the English alphabet. Although they can appear in upper- and lowercase forms, as well as in various fonts, the task of knowing letters is a constrained one—there are twenty-six! The limited universe of letters, and even their sound correspondences and combinations (forty-four sounds in total, represented by approximately 250 different spellings; Ball and Blachman 1991; Reed 2012) means that we teach for mastery. And, as previously discussed, when it comes to code-based literacy competencies, many of our ELs readily reach similar levels as their English-only peers (August and Shanahan 2006; Betts et al. 2009; Geva and Yaghoub Zadeh 2006; Jean and Geva 2009; Lesaux, Rupp, and Siegel 2007; Mancilla-Martinez and Lesaux 2011).

Meaning-based competencies, unlike their discrete code-based counterparts, are never checked off our list. Instead, they develop over the course of a lifetime. Because of how meaning-based skills develop, some researchers, like Nell Duke and Joanne Carlisle (2011), call them *growth constructs*. For these reasons, we know that many ELs need significantly more opportunities to develop meaning-based competencies than they currently receive. We also know that developing these competencies is a (long) journey, not a destination. That's why, when we create learning opportunities targeting these competencies, we need to remind ourselves that knowledge development is a process—it's about *growth* not *mastery*. When we approach a process-based construct with a mastery-oriented mind-set, we shortchange our students and, in so doing, often create frustrating teaching experiences for ourselves (e.g., lessons that take a lot of preparation but don't result in the kind of learning we had hoped for). So instead of pushing students to master words or subject matter through memorization or lockstep procedures, we take an approach that focuses on the learning process: grappling with ideas, reconciling inconsistencies, arriving at conclusions, and even making (and learning from) mistakes. In the knowledge-building classroom, personal and group achievements are celebrated, including the process of trial and error and practice. Cultivating knowledge is not achieved in one shot, and learning breakthroughs and milestones are not always readily visible.

What does this look like in Ms. Parkin's classroom?

A process-oriented approach looks and feels different from one that is mastery-oriented. Let's zero in on the way Ms. Parkin is teaching academic vocabulary, specifically, the word *disguise*. First, keep in mind that this lesson is situated within a multiunit sequence for building up word knowledge: Javier, Camilla, and their classmates encountered and used the word *disguise* in a previous unit focused on overcoming obstacles and are now gaining further understanding of this concept in the current, science-focused unit. In this way, Ms. Parkin's students are not merely committing a simple definition of *disguise* to memory but are working through how to use the concept in academic conversations, across contexts and content areas, over time.

What's more, because Ms. Parkin purposefully designed these units to relate to each other conceptually, she is providing students with the time and space needed for the knowledge-development journey. This includes the trial-and-error learning opportunities needed to move from narrow, context-bound word knowledge to rich, flexible word knowledge (see Figure 3.2). What does this mean for Javier? Well, when he contributes to the class discussion of the text, explaining that the "caterpillar is a disguise," he is trying out his emerging academic language skills. His response offers Ms. Parkin a window into his progress but also shows her that, when it comes to incorporating the term *disguise* smoothly and accurately into his academic talk, he's not quite there. But that's okay; within a process-oriented approach, Ms. Parkin can respond in this teachable moment with supportive feedback, but also, as the unit progresses, she will have plenty of chances to support Javier to write and talk about animal adaptations using the notion of *disguise* with more accuracy.

Within a mastery-oriented approach, on the other hand, *disguise* would likely have appeared on a list of words to be memorized that week, and in that time

SPOTLIGHT ON COLLEGE AND CAREER READINESS ENGLISH LANGUAGE ARTS STANDARDS AND THE ROLE OF PROCESS

A focus on the literacy learning process is embedded in the design of the CCSS, primarily through the English language arts Anchor Standards, which span grade levels and define the skills and understandings that all students must demonstrate (Common Core State Standards Initiative 2010). But they are not mastery-oriented. These Anchor Standards map out the long journey of preparing

frame, Javier might memorize the word's definition (at least for the short term), and maybe even learn a few synonyms and antonyms by heart, but not much more. In turn, Javier would not have had the time or the varied opportunities needed to develop a more conceptual understanding of the word, and Ms. Parkin would experience the challenge and potential frustration associated with trying to squeeze deep learning into a tight time frame.

Principle #3: Make learning interactive.

Instruction that cultivates knowledge (and therefore promotes advanced literacy development) is necessarily *interactive*. Research in the fields of cognitive psychology and the learning sciences make clear that learning, by its very nature, is social (National Scientific Council on the Developing Child 2009). From the earliest years, children's brains are designed for learning—this is why infants, toddlers, and children are always reaching out, in their amazingly individualized ways, for interaction. When adults initiate warm, supportive interactions or respond to children's initiations in this same way, and then keep the interaction going, children's knowledge develops. Children also support one another's learning when they interact with each other—classroom play is not just for fun; under many circumstances, it's cognitively stimulating! Interaction by interaction, unfamiliar words and content become meaningful and ultimately internalized.

We have all experienced the difference it makes in our learning when we have a back-and-forth conversation about something, rather than just hearing or reading about it on our own. Think about the last time you were trying to figure

for a productive career and engaged citizenship—one that is punctuated by grade-specific milestones along the way. We don't check these competencies off our list. Instead, we cultivate them. So, for example, teachers of writing, from grades K–12, are supporting their students to draw evidence from literary or informational texts to support analysis, reflection, and research (Writing Anchor Standard 9). No one teacher creates learning opportunities where this objective is mastered—no one teacher, in a single year, could! Instead, students grapple with what it means to support claims with evidence, and arrive at ways to generate evidence-based projects, throughout their school career (and even after that).

something out, or become more familiar with the unfamiliar, and you talked it through with a friend or colleague. Or think back to that high school class or a course at a college where the readings were difficult and dense but then came to life and made more sense when you discussed them in the classroom. In these instances, the dialogue, which might have been formal or informal, clarified your understanding of the issue and deepened your knowledge about something. Yet as a field, and especially when working with ELs, we don't do a very good job making the learning process interactive. This is a missed opportunity—we need to leverage the benefits of interaction in the service of improved outcomes, providing ELs with the interactive opportunities it takes to bring their literacy development to the next levels.

Also, remember that those literacy competencies that present a particular challenge for ELs are largely language-based: acquiring deep vocabulary knowledge, accumulating a deep understanding of academic concepts, and developing facility at expressing ideas about academic content. And yet, in many of our classrooms, we do much of the talking; we stand and deliver and expect that our students are learning. These lessons are most often well thought out, and students might well be listening. But deep learning requires an interactive experience. This is why we simply cannot expect ELs to increase their English language proficiency if we do not provide supportive, interactive spaces where they can be part of content-based conversations and purposeful play and above all have the chance to talk (and talk, and talk).

And so, knowledge-building classrooms are rarely quiet ones. Instead, educators in these classrooms recognize that building knowledge and promoting language development demands dialogue—and not just teacher talk. Daily practices in these classrooms include text-based discussions, oral presentations, debates, games, and questioning. These classrooms are not chaotic, but they include the buzz of productive noise. Still, for some, turning up the volume on classroom talk by providing daily opportunities to practice academic language in a meaningful, interactive way might feel like a tall order. In a crowded and busy classroom, it is easy to see how several conversations at once can feel (or even become) noisy and disordered. However, when the purpose and structure of discussion-based activities are part of students' learning routines, and these activities have developmentally appropriate time frames, the noise is productive and the disorder is fruitful.

What does this look like in Ms. Parkin's classroom?

Let's turn back to Ms. Parkin's classroom once again. In the opening of this chapter, Ms. Parkin is exposing her students to a rich, engaging informational text.

In and of itself, this reading is certainly worthwhile, but Ms. Parkin doesn't stop at this exposure to academic language. Instead, she poses a text-based question meant to focus students' attention on how the example in the text relates to their unit's big idea (Why does this rain forest caterpillar disguise itself, mimicking a snake?). Now, to quickly get a sense for students' understanding, she could pose this question and call on one of the raised hands for a response, listening to and evaluating that single response as right or wrong, and then move on. This is a common practice during classroom read-alouds; and it is not without some value, but this conversation routine does not leverage the benefits of interaction in the service of deeper learning. To accomplish that, Ms. Parkin needs to set up the kind of back-and-forth conversations that are central to deeper learning. And that is exactly what she does. Her students have learned and practiced the tried-and-true classroom conversation protocol think-pair-share. As a result, learning through conversation with their peers is central to daily classroom work. Javier, Camilla, and their classmates regularly try on academic language for size, experiment with this register of English in a safe and supportive environment, and do so purposefully in conversation about a text. Because of this regularity, this classroom scenario is not particularly elaborate or time-consuming. Interaction by interaction, Ms. Parkin's students move beyond surface-level understandings (a good starting place, definitely) to deeper, lasting learning.

SPOTLIGHT ON COLLEGE AND CAREER READINESS ENGLISH LANGUAGE ARTS STANDARDS AND THE ROLE OF INTERACTIVE LEARNING

Interaction is a key mechanism for building deep knowledge and for promoting ELs' oral communication competencies. The many skills required for academic talk are represented in the Listening and Speaking standards put forth by the CCSS and other college and career readiness standards (Common Core State Standards Initiative 2010). These standards remind us that the ability to engage in learning-focused interactions is a crucial goal in its own right. For example, Anchor Standard 1 states that students should be able to "prepare for and participate effectively in a range of conversations and

— continues —

— continued —

collaborations with diverse partners, building on others' ideas and expressing their own clearly and persuasively." Anchor Standard 4 similarly highlights the importance of interactive teaching and learning: Students should be able to present information, findings, and supporting evidence such that listeners can follow the line of reasoning and the organization, development, and style are appropriate to task, purpose, and audience.

How will ELs and their peers develop their skills as collaborators, debaters, and presenters without the context of supportive interactions where they have the chance to talk? Meeting these standards, and others like them, demands that teachers provide students with multiple opportunities to learn through discussion, debate points of view, and comprehensibly articulate their ideas. These standards implore us to turn up the volume!

Knowledge-Building Literacy Instruction: Making It Happen

Actual instructional strategies that accomplish these three principles—and together make for a knowledge-building classroom—are the focus of the remainder of this book. Remember, these principles are meant to guide instructional planning and act as guideposts for daily practice. Providing deep, process-oriented, and interactive learning opportunities requires a structure, content, and strategies. Figure 3.3 features a framework for the knowledge-building classroom. In what follows, we provide a brief overview of each strategy included in this framework. Then, in the remaining chapters of this book, we go into detail about how to put these strategies into action.

Provide consistency by organizing lessons within a knowledge-building cycle.

The first strategy that makes for a knowledge-building classroom focuses on the use of a regular, repeated lesson sequence, which provides an architecture for literacy instruction. In this consistent lesson sequence—what we are calling a "knowledge-building instructional cycle"—core learning tasks stay largely

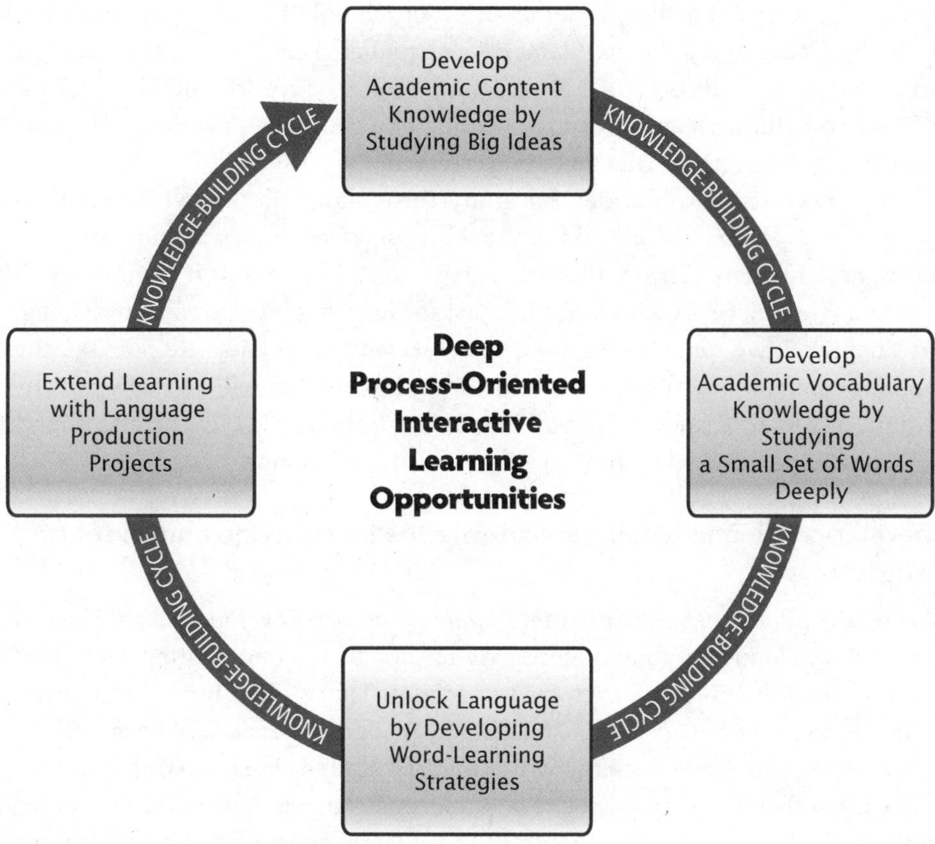

Figure 3.3 Knowledge-Building Instructional Framework

the same, but from cycle to cycle the content under focus changes. A knowledge-building cycle provides ELs and their monolingual English-speaking peers with the consistency and predictability needed to master the expectations and procedures, to focus on the content at hand—content that should at once be accessible, challenging, and engaging. Discussed more in Chapter 4, we should be clear that not every instructional cycle is a knowledge-building one; that chapter outlines the elements of a knowledge-building cycle.

Develop academic content knowledge by studying big ideas.

A knowledge-building instructional cycle has a big idea woven throughout and as a result is set up to focus on deep learning. This sustained content focus is what makes the instructional cycle shine—it's a crucial platform for advancing each EL's knowledge and therefore literacy development. Text plays an important role in the study of each big idea. Most often, we introduce the big idea and kick off the cycle through an interactive reading of a complex, engaging, discussion-worthy text that features the topic to be studied.

When selecting a big idea for study throughout the knowledge-building cycle, the key is to ensure it's big enough to come back to again and again—that we're able to study it from different perspectives and look at it from many different angles, all of which matter not just for learning but also for engagement. In Chapter 5, we dig into what big ideas are and what they are not. We then answer common questions about how to select texts that will be really effective within this kind of knowledge-building instructional cycle but will also support ELs, including those who are struggling to read for meaning.

Develop academic vocabulary knowledge by studying a small set of words deeply.

Many ELs require significantly more opportunities to develop the sophisticated, abstract, academic vocabulary necessary to support reading, writing, and discussion of the academic topics covered in school. That's why, in this approach to literacy instruction, we study a small set of academic vocabulary terms. By *academic vocabulary*, we mean those words that are used in classrooms and text much more often than in everyday social and informal settings (Baker et al. 2014). You might ask: If our goal is to increase ELs' academic vocabulary knowledge, why study only a small set of words?

Well, if we are going to accomplish our goal of teaching that results in advanced literacy skills, then it's only feasible and sensible to move away from shallow coverage. Bear in mind that many of our ELs and their classmates have *some* knowledge of many academic words, but that knowledge is not deep enough to support text comprehension or their use of the words in their academic writing. So, if we start with fewer words and devote more time to studying them, students will have the opportunity to learn concepts and nuances associated with a given word (i.e., deep learning!) and a chance to practice using words through writing, speaking, and listening activities in the classroom (i.e., interactive learning!). In Chapter 6, we focus on how to choose words wisely and illustrate what this selection process looks like.

Unlock language by developing word-learning strategies.

As they progress through school, our students encounter a large number of words that are unfamiliar to them. And it's just not possible to provide them with direct instruction in *all* of the words they may not be familiar with. Or, in other words, teaching them the roughly 50,000 words they need to know by the end of high school is too big a job. But what we can do is turn them into good word learners—we can arm them with the tools and skills to unlock the meaning of unfamiliar words. Therefore, the next element of knowledge-building literacy instruction is a focus on word-learning skills. How can classroom instruction help unlock language for students, equipping our ELs, especially, to be expert word learners? It can focus on helping students to:

- break words into meaningful parts
- use clues found in surrounding text
- tune in to the words around them
- make connections to their native language.

In Chapter 7, we illustrate what it looks like to develop ELs' word-learning strategies, focusing on the cognitive steps and morphological knowledge it takes to unlock language.

Extend learning with language production projects.

Last but most definitely not least, we turn to a strategy that's probably the most neglected but is key to creating a knowledge-building classroom: extending learning with language production projects. Although not enacted very frequently, these projects can often take the form of capstones, offering students the opportunity to consolidate and extend their understanding of the content studied over the course of the instructional cycle. Depending on the cycle's big idea and students' developmental stage, a language production project might take the form of a debate, letter-writing campaign, public service announcement, mock trial, or presentation. Whether the project primarily involves oral or written language, students work on these projects over an extended period of time, drawing on their cumulative knowledge. (Note: This is very different from "daily oral language" activities!) Through the multiday process of planning and generating a written or spoken product, ELs develop the academic language skills that will support learning and development across the domains of literacy and across the content areas. Language production projects extend ELs' learning when they:

- are anchored projects in the cycle's big idea
- encourage and support use of target vocabulary terms
- provide a compelling reason to complete the project (e.g., communicating with an audience students really want to connect with and/or addressing an aspect of the cycle's big idea that students really care about).

But designing a knowledge-building language production project is only the first step. Next, we must build in the supports ELs need to reach our high expectations. How can teachers support ELs as they work on projects in which they communicate their expertise through purposeful and meaningful writing, presentation, or debate? They can do so by employing instructional tools designed to scaffold the process of crafting language-based projects. In Chapter 8, we describe the whys, whats, and how-tos of extending learning with language production projects.

Bringing It All Together

Let's return one last time to Ms. Parkin and her third-grade class. By organizing instruction around a big question (i.e., How do animals survive in their environments?), anchoring the study of this question in a content-rich and engaging text (e.g., *Butterflies and Moths*, by Nic Bishop), and studying high-impact academic words (e.g., *disguise, survive, environment*) across weeks and content areas, she was enacting the three principles outlined here and bringing them to life using some of the strategies we highlight that make knowledge-building instruction happen. In designing her instruction this way, Ms. Parkin avoids a few common pitfalls, depicted and described in Figure 3.4. When our teaching takes this approach and similarly sidesteps these pitfalls, striving toward building ELs' knowledge, we place our students on a path toward reaching their full academic potential.

Common Pitfalls to Avoid	Shifts in the Knowledge-Building Classroom	How?
Lessons "cover" lots of topics, exposing students to many (often unconnected) concepts.	Learning is organized around a big idea so that students engage in the process of coming back to a multifaceted topic again and again—deepening understanding.	Sequence lessons within a knowledge-building instructional cycle (Chapter 4) that is organized around a big idea (Chapter 5).
Lists of words are memorized each week and "daily oral language" activities occur outside of content learning.	Language learning is part of an extended and meaningful process: The study of words and concepts is anchored in big ideas, texts, classroom talk, and language production projects.	Choose a small set of words from a content-rich text, study those words deeply (Chapter 6), and then use them to develop an extended, written or oral project (Chapter 8).
Learning activities involve sitting and listening, independent seat work, and the occasional turn-and-talk.	Dialogue, debate, and questioning are central to learning: Lots of teacher-to-student and student-to-student interaction makes for noisier, busier, and more effective learning activities.	Use content-based conversations and guided word play to practice and internalize word meanings, word transformations (Chapter 7), and communication skills (Chapter 8).

Figure 3.4 Bringing It All Together: Deep, Process-Oriented, and Interactive Learning

PROTOCOLS FOR PLANNING AND REFLECTION

Deep, Process-Oriented, and Interactive Learning Opportunities in My Classroom

Begin filling in this table by recording your initial brainstorms, based on Chapter 3. Then, as you read subsequent chapters, add ideas and strategies to your lists.

Instructional Principles for the Knowledge-Building Classroom	***What strategies and activities do I already use that accomplish this principle?***	***What other strategies or activities might I incorporate into my instruction to further accomplish this principle?***
Go for Depth of Learning Take a "less-is-more" approach, focusing on the study of concepts, words, and questions from several angles.		
Focus on the Learning Process Go for growth over mastery, providing multiple, meaningful opportunities for ELs to grapple with ideas, arrive at conclusions, change their opinions, and make (and learn from) mistakes.		
Make Learning Interactive Weave opportunities into instructional activities for students to have content-focused, back-and-forth conversations with one another.		

Provide Consistency by Organizing Lessons Within a Cycle

Sitting with her guided reading group, Ms. Parkin briefly scans the room, visually "taking the pulse," as she likes to think, of the behavior and engagement levels of her bustling third graders. She's only just retrieved the leveled readers and word sort cards for her group, but in these few minutes the rest of the class has already settled into their work. Based on yesterday's lesson and the stage of this knowledge-building cycle—on how animals survive in their environment—her students know what to expect today: In pairs, they are to carry out interviews with each other, one playing the role of the scientist who was discussed in yesterday's read-aloud and the other asking questions, using some of the words they've been studying. To help them along, each pair has a familiar toolkit to support them: sample interview questions with sentence starters for responses; a relevant excerpt from yesterday's read-aloud; and a log book for the interviewer to write notes afterward. As she finishes scanning the room, Ms. Parkin overhears Javier and Mateo, a pair that probably took the longest to get to this independent stage, going over the plan and routine as they get started. "How rewarding," Ms. Parkin thinks to herself, "to see these third-grade learners in action." She turns toward her reading group and begins to introduce their new book.

To set English learners (ELs) up to build knowledge about a big idea, we have to minimize the daily class time spent on having students learn new instructional tasks and activities. A knowledge-building cycle—like the one Javier and Mateo are in the midst of—does just that. It provides the framework for deep learning and the support students need to get there. It is therefore a powerful tool for designing learning environments that are at once demanding and supportive—learning environments where doable challenges are part of the everyday and both academic learning and motivation are strengthened. The knowledge-building cycle is a sequence of lessons that are made up of core learning tasks, designed to be used for any and all big ideas; these core learning tasks, the majority of which are interactive, repeat from cycle to cycle (see Figure 4.1).

How Does an Instructional Cycle Support Deeper Learning?

When we only occasionally implement an activity that involves language production and student interaction, multiple steps, or both, many ELs and their classroom peers are too bogged down trying to remember and get comfortable with *how* to carry out the assignment. They may be off-task and their teachers may be

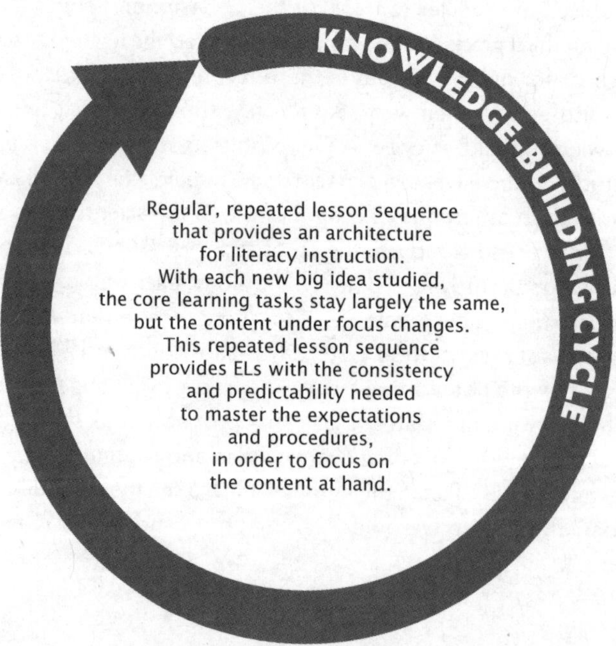

KNOWLEDGE-BUILDING CYCLE
Regular, repeated lesson sequence that provides an architecture for literacy instruction. With each new big idea studied, the core learning tasks stay largely the same, but the content under focus changes. This repeated lesson sequence provides ELs with the consistency and predictability needed to master the expectations and procedures, in order to focus on the content at hand.

Figure 4.1 What is a knowledge-building cycle?

increasingly frustrated. On the surface, it might seem like it makes good sense to do this challenging activity only on those days that you've mustered up the professional stamina, otherwise limiting everyday learning tasks to those that are less challenging. But by not engaging our ELs in these specific tasks with regularity and frequency, we've set it up so that they are even less likely to gain familiarity and ease with the steps and expectations—and we don't get the click or hum that Ms. Parkin is enjoying and the deep learning we see in action. Point being: We need to create the conditions necessary for ELs to gain competence with the kinds of interactive, content-based activities they need to engage in if they are going to develop advanced literacy skills.

Taking a knowledge-building approach to literacy instruction, we bring the world to ELs in meaningful ways, supporting them to develop the academic knowledge and language they need to access and generate a range of texts now and as they grow up. Thinking back to the three key principles of this approach, described in detail in Chapter 3, brings us to the need for an intentional, consistent plan that facilitates deep, process-oriented, and interactive learning environments (see Figure 4.2). A plan that combats the challenge of getting students like

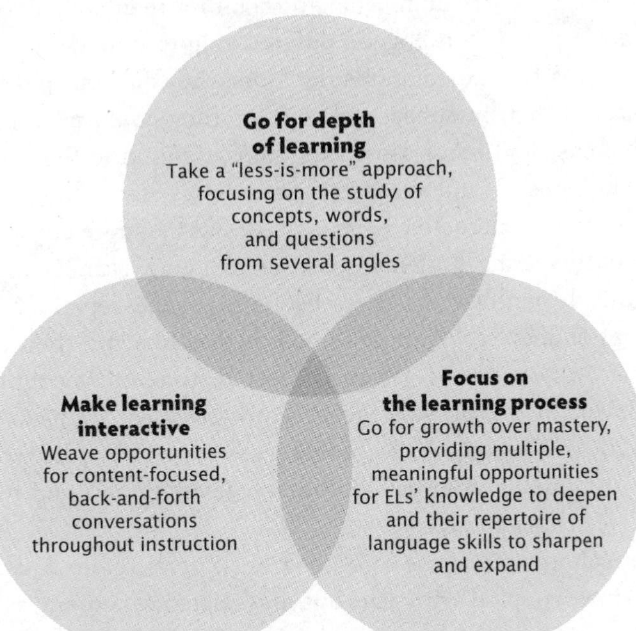

Figure 4.2 Chapter 3 Recap: Principles of Knowledge-Building Literacy Instruction

Javier and Mateo to a place where they can regularly engage in interactive, content-based, day-to-day learning tasks that promote their advanced literacy skills. What kind of plan is needed? It likely comes as no surprise: Our own research and that of others shows that consistent day-to-day and cycle-to-cycle lesson structures are instrumental in making rigorous content engaging and accessible rather than discouraging and prohibitive (Kern and Clemens 2007; Lesaux, Harris, and Sloane 2012). This research confirms what so many teachers already knew: Instructional consistency is foundational to accomplishing our goals for deep learning.

For example, in a study we conducted in a linguistically diverse urban school district in the southwest United States, fifth- and sixth-grade teachers serving large numbers of ELs and struggling readers in elementary and middle schools implemented an approach that exemplifies the principles and strategies we are describing in this book. The curriculum we tested focuses on building up students' concept and word knowledge in the context of two-week knowledge-building cycles—each organized around a big idea and a set of high-utility academic vocabulary words. As part of the cycle, students engage in collaborative learning tasks that involve writing, structured discussions, and morphology-focused activities using the target vocabulary. Initially, this was very challenging for all. Many teachers perceived the curriculum as too difficult for their students, and students told us that, at first, they felt bogged down trying to understand the very new kinds of procedures and expectations, let alone the concepts and language. But students explained that, in subsequent cycles, they could move through tasks with increasing ease and focus, directing their attention to their developing literacy skills. This sense of increased competence was rewarding in and of itself and made challenging, interactive learning tasks all the more engaging (Lesaux et al. 2012). For participating students, when challenging learning activities cycled from unit to unit, as part of a consistent lesson sequence, repetition was anything but rote—it was supportive! And, it's not just that ELs and their peers *felt* like it was working. In fact, it was. When we tested students' vocabulary, reading, and writing development, we saw the very progress that students told us about (Lesaux et al. 2014). The knowledge-building cycle was a key ingredient in accelerating these students' academic vocabulary development and fostering their growing sense of academic success.

This study, along with those of other researchers, reminds us that instructional consistency, coupled with rigorous and engaging content, isn't a strategy that solely supports ELs' learning—it also benefits monolingual English speakers. This overlap is no small matter. So many educators across the United States, just like Ms. Parkin and the teachers in our study, are teaching in schools populated by linguistically diverse students—classrooms filled with students who speak a language other than English at home and students who speak English at home, as well as many students who speak a combination of languages at home. Therefore, when we craft our evidence-based guidance, we think very carefully about instructional strategies that are important for ELs but also have the potential to benefit all of the members of a classroom community. A knowledge-building cycle is a platform for doing just that.

How Do I Design a Knowledge-Building Cycle?

Just any repeated sequence of core learning tasks won't necessarily result in a *knowledge-building* learning environment. In our research and our collaboration with teachers, we have learned five key features of knowledge-building instructional cycles. Incorporate these features when designing a cycle that will work for you and your students. We list these features here and then unpack them in the sections that follow, providing examples from Ms. Parkin's classroom.

1. Identify and then repeat core learning tasks from cycle to cycle so that ELs and their peers can master the routines and expectations.
2. Sequence core learning tasks developmentally so that ELs and their peers can continue to engage in the incremental process of developing knowledge and language.
3. Continue to advance students' literacy development by gradually increasing the cognitive and linguistic demands of the core learning tasks as the year progresses.
4. Provide ELs and their peers with opportunities to study academic words and concepts using multiple methods and formats.
5. Organize each instructional cycle around a big idea or question to support the goal of deep learning.

1. Identify and then repeat core learning tasks from cycle to cycle so that ELs and their peers can master the routines and expectations.

In a knowledge-building classroom, a core set of learning tasks should recur from cycle to cycle, enabling students to gain familiarity and ease with the expectations and processes associated with those activities. This repetition, however, is anything but rote! On the contrary, predictable procedures and activities are actually a way to help learners engage even more in the kind of thinking, talking, and writing that takes them out of the here and now. When learning tasks are familiar, ELs and their peers are freed up to focus on each cycle's big idea.

WHEN STUDENT-FRIENDLY REPETITION CAN FEEL NOT-SO-TEACHER-FRIENDLY

In our own research in partnership with teachers, we learned that for some, the repetition and consistency required for a knowledge-building instructional cycle felt satisfying and rewarding because these teachers could see the repetition and consistency working for their students. One teacher told us, "I know that kids need several times to practice, and [this approach] provides that for them so that they can get better and better . . . It's something that they don't get through the other [approaches], sort of like, 'Do a little bit of this, and now we're going to change and do this, and then we're going to do something else.' "

But for other teachers, the repetition was an instructional challenge. Some had a hard time sticking with it, and others were concerned about the engagement of their higher-performing students, mistaking instructional consistency for rote, monotonous instruction. One teacher linked the repeated cycle to his own "focus wandering" and wanted to "pick up the pace."

We can relate to both perspectives—we've been there ourselves! But the research and our practical experience, at scale, tell us that, when we stick with it, an instructional cycle affords student engagement rather than impedes it. Going deep on topics and using similar structures for conversations, time and again, makes for deep learning and high levels of engagement. We also know that, when it *does* work for teachers, it's a key ingredient in accelerating ELs' language and literacy development. So, what advice do we have for the reticent teacher?

1. Take your time at first—allow students to learn the expectations and process.
2. Stick with it—a quality routine isn't boring, it's supportive!
3. Over time, make changes to the routine that are responsive to ELs' learning and growth—when we continue to tweak a routine, raising the bar by decreasing scaffolding and increasing complexity, it's never rote.

What does this look like in Ms. Parkin's classroom?

As described in Figure 4.3, in each knowledge-building cycle, Ms. Parkin returns to several interactive core learning tasks. Some of these tasks are part of her school's curriculum (e.g., think-pair-share), and she learned others (e.g., interactive crossword puzzles) through professional development and still others (e.g., "praise, question, suggest") through collaboration with her colleagues teaching higher grade levels. She latched on to these additions because she finds that they complement the existing curriculum nicely, adding depth to those areas where

Core Learning Task	**Procedure**	**How Does Ms. Parkin Use It?**
Think-Pair-Share: A Discussion Routine	A question or prompt is posed. Then students: ▪ *think*, independently formulating their ideas during a brief and specific time frame (e.g., 1 minute) ▪ *pair*, sharing their thinking with a peer and listening to their peer's ideas (~1–2 minutes each) ▪ *share*, participating in a whole-group discussion about partners' conversations.	Ms. Parkin uses this discussion routine during read-alouds; therefore, this is a learning task at multiple points in the instructional cycle. She poses text-based questions and provides students with supports for their responses (e.g., sentence starters). As the year progresses, she also sets parameters to increase the challenge of the task (e.g., encouraging students to use evidence to support their ideas).
Carousel Brainstorm: A Collaborative Learning Routine	Questions, issues, or target vocabulary words are listed on separate pieces of chart paper and posted around the room. Students are split into small groups, each with a different-color marker, and assigned to an initial chart paper station. Then, in these small groups, students: ▪ collaboratively brainstorm and record their responses to the prompt. This happens briefly, within a specific time frame (e.g., after 2 minutes, a timer beeps) ▪ move to the next chart paper station and brainstorm responses to the listed prompt; this "carousel" around the room continues until each group has visited all stations ▪ come back together as a whole group, engaging in a teacher-facilitated discussion of their postings.	Typically, Ms. Parkin uses this cooperative learning routine twice per cycle. First, she uses it as a way for students to brainstorm their background knowledge about the cycle's target words—this provides a gauge of students' current understandings and she can immediately clarify any confusion. Toward the end of the cycle, she posts questions related to the cycle's big idea and corresponding texts, prompting her students to integrate and/or consolidate what they are learning.

continues

Figure 4.3 Core Learning Tasks: Examples from Ms. Parkin's Classroom

Core Learning Task	Procedure	How Does Ms. Parkin Use It?
Interactive Crossword Puzzle: Partner Learning Game	Each player has a copy of a crossword puzzle with half of the answers already filled into the blocks. One student has all of the "down" answers filled in, and the other has all of the "across" answers filled in. Taking turns, students follow the following procedure: ▪ The first student provides clues so that her partner can figure out one of the "down" answers. ▪ The second student provides clues so that his partner can figure out one of the "across" answers. ▪ Students continue to take turns until both players have a complete puzzle.	Ms. Parkin uses this game as a literacy center. Most often, the cycle's target words are featured in the puzzles. To make the puzzles, Ms. Parkin goes to a free online crossword puzzle maker and enters all the target words. She leaves the clues blank. Then, she prints two copies of the puzzle. She then fills in the down answers on one copy and fills in the across answers on the other. These half-filled-in puzzles can then be photocopied—and there you have it—an Interactive Crossword Puzzle: Partner Learning Game! (It's a hit in the classrooms we work in—and a great learning task!)
Mock Interview: Paired Discussion Activity	Each student has a copy of the same question sheet featuring a list of interview questions. Using these, students: ▪ (if choice is provided) select the role they would like to play when they are interviewed ▪ select the questions they would like to be asked, marking those questions on their page (e.g., choosing two out of the four questions listed) ▪ interview each other guided by their partner's selected questions.	Ms. Parkin uses this partner discussion activity as a way to support students to apply both their developing *academic vocabulary knowledge* and their developing knowledge about the *cycle's big idea*. In each cycle, the interview questions feature the target words and the scenario for the interview relates to a text that was read aloud. To promote word analysis, sometimes the target words take a different morphological form (e.g., a prefix or suffix added).
Praise, Question, Suggest: A Partner Revision Routine	In pairs, students read and explain their written text; one person shares and the other listens and provides feedback, and vice versa. The active listener: ▪ *praises* at least one specific element of the text ▪ *asks a question*, such as a question about the author's ideas, choices, or writing process ▪ *suggests a revision*, such as something she might add, change, or clarify.	Ms. Parkin uses this routine to support the writing process. She finds it requires a good deal of modeling and practicing, but it's worth the effort. The fourth- and fifth-grade teachers at her school use this routine too, to provide students with instructional consistency. In addition to the work on the writing process, she finds that teaching and practicing this routine provides a rich opportunity for students to further develop their interpersonal communication skills, such as communicating clearly, listening actively, considering their peers' perspectives, and managing their emotional responses.

Figure 4.3 Core Learning Tasks: Examples from Ms. Parkin's Classroom *(continued)*

her students need intensive learning opportunities all the while setting them up to be successful with routines and approaches they will encounter in fourth and fifth grades.

During the first several knowledge-building cycles, Ms. Parkin allots a good chunk of time to explicitly teaching the steps involved in each of these core learning tasks and modeling what it looks like to move through these steps. Still, at the beginning, as students move through these tasks independently, the procedures feel more clunky than efficient. Her students require explicit reminders regarding how to accomplish each task, such as visuals with the steps posted on the wall and additional modeling and guidance. But several cycles into the year, even when the tasks involve different questions, words, and concepts, Ms. Parkin's students are able to carry out the activities productively: They have a handle on the procedures and can fully take advantage of the opportunity to practice their academic language skills.

THE RESEARCH ABOUT CYCLE LENGTH

There is no hard-and-fast, research-based rule regarding the precise number of days or weeks to allocate to each knowledge-building cycle. Ultimately, as long as you are bringing the principles of knowledge-building instruction to bear, the exact length of your cycle depends upon your students' developmental stages, the curriculum and resources in place, and your professional insights into other contextual factors.

That being said, existing research does provide examples of what might work (Carlo et al. 2004; Hickman, Pollard-Durodola, and Vaughn 2004; Lesaux, Kieffer et al. 2010; Silverman and Hines 2009). Based on this research, we think it makes good sense to design a knowledge-building cycle that comprises 2–4 weeks' worth of lessons and corresponding core learning tasks, each of which is organized around one big idea and corresponding touchstone text (Chapter 5) and a set of high-utility academic words (Chapter 6). For some classrooms, each cycle will involve the study of a new big idea, and in others, several cycles will be linked together, each focused on a different facet of a big idea, making for a larger unit of study.

2. Sequence core learning tasks developmentally so that ELs and their peers can continue to engage in the incremental process of developing knowledge and language.

When designing a knowledge-building cycle, it is also important to think very intentionally about *how* core activities are sequenced to promote development. Figure 4.4 provides a bird's-eye view of how we think about sequencing lessons within a knowledge-building cycle to match the incremental process of building knowledge and language. Using this developmental sequence as a guide, you might begin each cycle with a content-based shared experience (e.g., demonstration or video clip) and the reading of the cycle's touchstone text (see Chapter 5) to

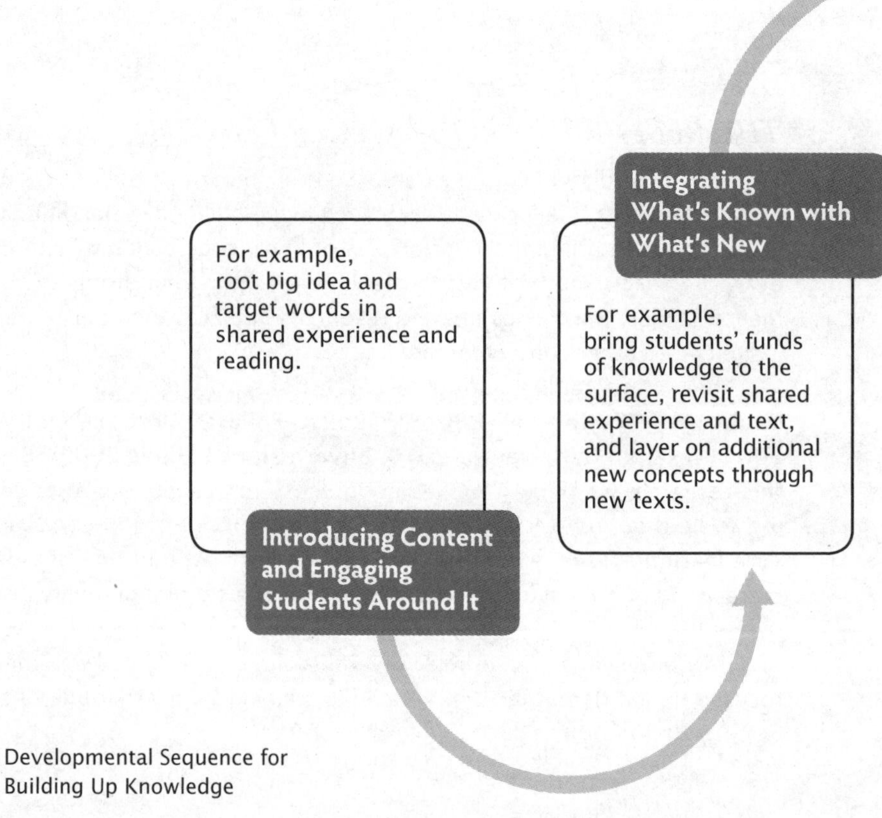

For example,
root big idea and
target words in a
shared experience and
reading.
Introducing Content
and Engaging
Students Around It
Integrating
What's Known with
What's New
For example,
bring students' funds
of knowledge to the
surface, revisit shared
experience and text,
and layer on additional
new concepts through
new texts.

Figure 4.4 Developmental Sequence for Building Up Knowledge

introduce the big idea and engage students around it (Baker et al. 2014). Through subsequent activities, you might then support ELs to connect their relevant background knowledge to what they are learning and then begin to layer on additional, related concepts through revisiting the touchstone text and reading other texts. As the cycle continues, it would then be useful to provide ELs with new contexts, experiences, and formats to talk and write about the cycle's big idea and to try academic language on for size. Finally, to extend what's known to produce a message, each cycle might conclude with a language production project: Depending on the topic and grade level, this language production project might take the form of a debate, letter-writing campaign, public service announcement, mock trial, or presentation (Chapter 8).

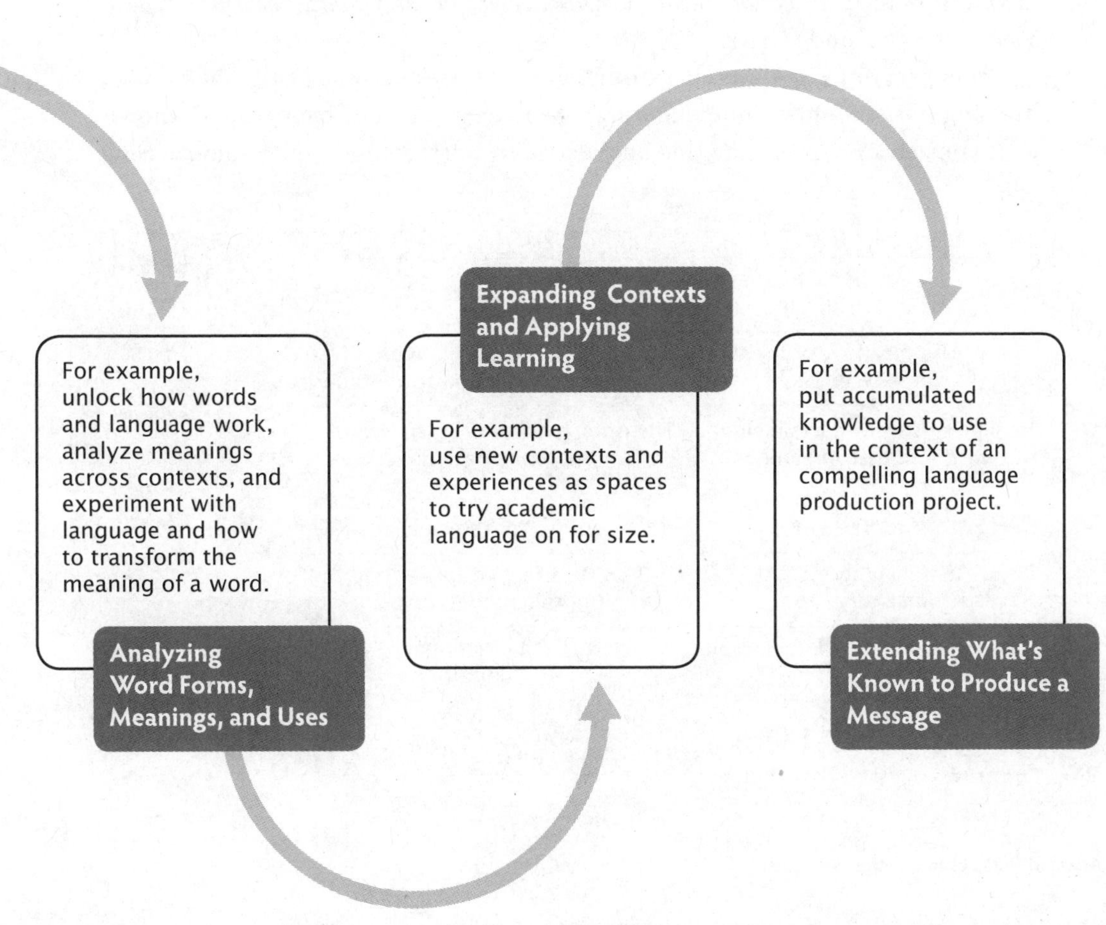

For example, unlock how words and language work, analyze meanings across contexts, and experiment with language and how to transform the meaning of a word.
Analyzing Word Forms, Meanings, and Uses
Expanding Contexts and Applying Learning
For example, use new contexts and experiences as spaces to try academic language on for size.
For example, put accumulated knowledge to use in the context of an compelling language production project.
Extending What's Known to Produce a Message

What does this look like in Ms. Parkin's classroom?

When sequencing the core learning tasks in her knowledge-building cycle, Ms. Parkin paid particular attention to building up vocabulary knowledge incrementally. Figure 4.5 lays out her sequence and how it builds up vocabulary knowledge over the course of a nine-day knowledge-building cycle. On day 1 of her cycle, Ms. Parkin provides a foundation, building her students' receptive vocabulary knowledge through an interactive reading of the cycle's touchstone text and then introducing the target words explicitly. For example, to launch the current cycle, focused on how animals survive in their environments, Ms. Parkin reads *Why Do Tigers Have Stripes?* by Mike Unwin. After reading and discussing this informational book, Ms. Parkin introduces the cycle's target words—concepts drawn from the text: *adapt*, *attract*, *disguise*, *environment*, *pattern*, *recognize*, *reflect*, *shadow*, *surface*, and *survive.*

Then, on days 2–4, Ms. Parkin integrates what's known with what's new: drawing out students' understanding, learning what their background knowledge consists of, connecting this knowledge to classroom learning, and revising

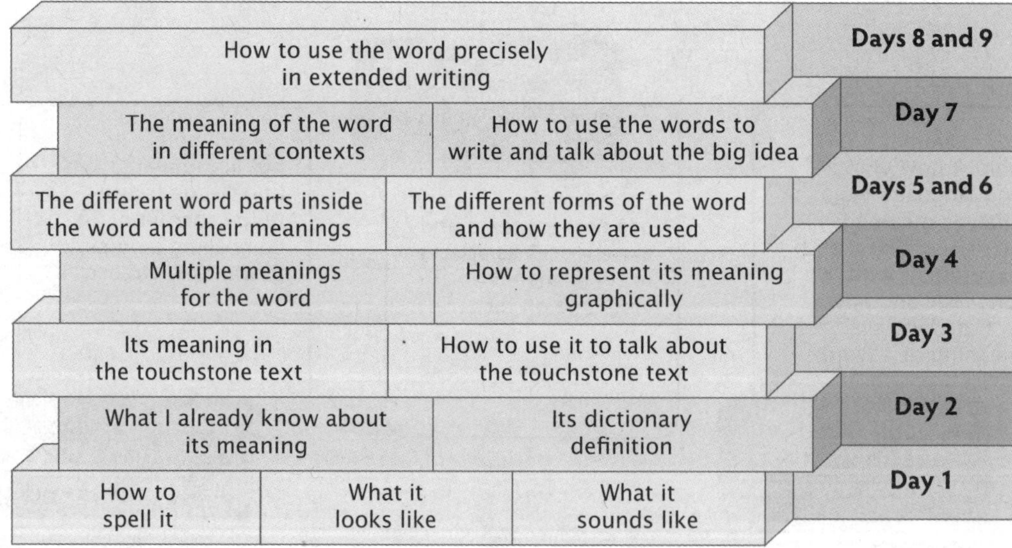

Adapted from Lesaux, Kieffer et al. 2010

Figure 4.5 Ms. Parkin's Sequence for Developing Academic Vocabulary Knowledge

misunderstandings. This step necessarily involves direct instruction of word meanings, but also *lots* of talk and writing: Students engage in the "carousel brainstorm" routine described in Figure 4.3, talking together about what they know about each word's usage and meaning. Then, after a whole-group discussion during which students' background knowledge is compared to a student-friendly dictionary definition, students generate their own definitions and pictures that represent those definitions.

In this first half of her knowledge-building cycle, Ms. Parkin further cultivates students' understanding of the target words by revisiting familiar texts (e.g., the touchstone text) and by layering on the reading of new texts and other language experiences that relate to the words. For example, early on in this particular cycle, Ms. Parkin and her students revisit *Why Do Tigers Have Stripes?* but then the class also reads and discusses Nic Bishop's *Butterflies and Moths* as well as the first section of a *Time for Kids* article about how elephants survive in their environment and the role that they play in their overall habitat. Students use the cycle's target words when discussing these texts as a whole group and during partner and center activities that build off of these texts and the content they convey, such as the mock interview discussion activity described in the chapter's opening—the interviews that Javier and Mateo are conducting.

At the midpoint of her knowledge-building cycle, on days 5–6, Ms. Parkin carves out the time to focus explicitly on analyzing and applying multiple word meanings and forms, paying particular attention to developing her students' morphological awareness. In the current cycle, together, they focus on the suffix *-able*, learning how to transform words using this suffix (e.g., *recognize* and *recognizable*) and using these new word forms in their writing (for more on this, see Chapter 7). Gradually, as the cycle progresses, Ms. Parkin supports students to produce language using these words. First, her students use the words when discussing or writing about familiar texts; then, on day 7, they try out these terms in new (albeit related) contexts. In this case, Ms. Parkin and her students read the latter half of the *Time for Kids* article about elephants and their natural environment, but this time focusing on the ways in which habitat loss and poaching influence this species' survival. Following this, students engage once more in the "carousel brainstorm" routine, now discussing the cycle's concepts of adaptation, survival, and environmental change. Ultimately, at the end of each cycle, Ms. Parkin extends her students' academic vocabulary knowledge by supporting and challenging them to generate a written product that communicates their emerging expertise and current thinking around the cycle's big idea (Chapter 8). When designing the final project for this knowledge-building cycle, Ms. Parkin aims to provide students with the opportunity to grapple with the issue of animal survival and environmental change: constructing their own points of view and expressing these perspectives to their community of learners.

In each cycle, this developmental sequencing enables students to move from a general sense or narrow, context-bound understanding of the cycle's target words to a rich, decontextualized understanding of the concept(s) these words represent. For example, in the current instructional cycle, Ms. Parkin aims to move students from knowing that adaptations (like camouflage and communication signals) help animals survive to an awareness of the many different physical and behavioral forms of adaptations; an understanding of the relationship between an organism's habitat and its adaptations; and an insight into how changes in an animal's habitat will influence how well suited its adaptations are for its survival.

3. Continue to advance students' literacy development by gradually increasing the cognitive and linguistic demands of the core learning tasks as the year progresses.

Because core tasks recur from unit to unit and students become more and more proficient with them, with time you can turn up the rigor. This doesn't mean changing the routine—if we did that, we'd lose the repetition that allows for deep learning and engagement. Instead, we mean purposefully and thoughtfully revising core tasks so that they are responsive to learners' development while maintaining their integrity so that students aren't learning completely new procedures and expectations. This responsive teaching can involve:

1. gradually removing scaffolding
2. adding complexity to activities
3. allowing students to take increasing responsibility for their learning.

Let's take the mock interview activity and think through what it might look like to gradually increase the rigor. As you might recall, in this particular speaking and listening activity, students work in pairs, each choosing a role to act out as their partner interviews them, using questions you provide. When first using this core learning task, you would likely provide a high level of linguistic and cognitive scaffolding so that students can gain ease with the associated steps and procedure. This support could take many forms:

- teaching the steps explicitly
- posting a visual that displays the steps

- modeling what it looks like to carry out the steps, using the same questions that students will respond to in their pairs
- debriefing the modeled steps while reflecting on the process and how to carry them out
- having students practice the procedure with an assigned partner, discussing questions that are minimally challenging, so that they can focus on the steps of this task
- providing sentence frames for responding (e.g., "I think ____________ because ____________").

This degree of scaffolding might be maintained over the course of the first several cycles. But then as students gain familiarity and ease with the procedure and expectations, your use of this activity in subsequent cycles can feature ramped-up cognitive and linguistic demands while providing fewer supports. Figure 4.6 illustrates how you might turn up the rigor of mock interviews.

What does this look like in Ms. Parkin's classroom?

Taking the think-pair-share procedure as the example, early in the year, Ms. Parkin poses the same or very similar questions each time (e.g., "What did you learn from this book?") and provides students with a sentence starter for responding to this question (e.g., "I learned that ____________"). Later in the year, when

Gradually remove scaffolding	Add complexity to the activity	Allow students to take increasing ownership of their learning
▪ Model how to respond to only one of the questions, rather than all of them. ▪ Shorten or take away sentence frames. ▪ Adjust your level of involvement, allowing students to work on their own as you circulate around the room.	▪ Tailor the questions to include more academic language and/or to push students to think more abstractly. ▪ Support and encourage students to provide additional reasoning or evidence for their answers or to take a stance on a multifaceted dilemma.	▪ Build in choice, allowing students to decide which questions to discuss. ▪ Involve students in the process of generating questions and sentence starters.

Figure 4.6 Ways to Turn Up the Rigor Using Mock Interview Partner Talk Activity

animal adaptation and survival are being studied, she poses questions that are much more specific to the text at hand, designing each question to match her content- and language-learning goals. She also increasingly requires that students use evidence to provide support for their responses. For example, during their second reading of the book *Why Do Tigers Have Stripes?* Ms. Parkin wants to support her students to begin to understand the relationship between the environment in which an animal lives and its adaptations. Therefore, after the section of the text describing animal disguises that help them to hide from prey and predators, she poses questions to match this learning goal: "What would happen if the leaf butterfly and the thorn bug traded places? How well would their disguises work in the other's environment?" When students discuss their responses, she expects them to use the cycle's target words as well as evidence from the book to support their ideas. In this case, a student might explain that a thorn bug has a thorn on its back that looks like a thorn on the branch that it lives; if the thorn bug lived where the leaf butterfly lives (on the orange and brown forest floor) its thorn would no longer be a disguise—the green and yellow patterns on the thorn would attract attention and no longer benefit the bug's survival.

4. Provide ELs and their peers with opportunities to study academic words and concepts using multiple methods and formats.

Throughout the instructional cycle, it is important to provide ELs and their peers with plenty of opportunities to learn about, question, and explore the concepts under study. When designing the instructional cycle, this means:

- **Use multiple instructional methods.** Balance direct, explicit instruction with inquiry-based (aka project-based) learning. For example, it is important to provide a healthy dose of learning opportunities that are grounded in explicit teaching, such as reviewing student-friendly definitions of words and explaining how to transform words by adding or taking away prefixes and suffixes. At the same time, students' learning is further enhanced when they experiment, play, and explore on their own and with peers in structured, scaffolded ways; for example, use literacy-enriched learning centers where ELs investigate books or artifacts related to the cycle's topic.
- **Target the different components of literacy.** Provide opportunities to build reading, writing, and speaking competencies. A knowledge-building instructional cycle includes structured, vocabulary-rich games; several thematically related readings; opportunities to produce short printed messages as well as extended writing projects; and varied oral language

activities, from quick think-pair-shares to extended and planned debates and presentations.

- **Vary instructional groupings.** To review, apply, and expand what they know, ELs need diverse learning experiences under different conditions. Be sure that ELs have the chance to build their knowledge in the context of convening as a whole class, meeting with similarly skilled students and also collaborating with peers at different stages, and, of course, working through content independently.

What does this look like in Ms. Parkin's classroom?

Throughout each cycle, and across the year, Ms. Parkin is sure to explicitly teach key concepts related to the cycle's big idea and target words, but she also provides opportunities for inquiry-based learning experiences in which students build up knowledge independently or in groups. These more inquiry-based learning opportunities include hands-on projects, scientific investigations, and surveys. For example, in this knowledge-building cycle focused on how animals survive in their environments, Ms. Parkin's students are examining a terrarium (from the science kit provided by her school), recording what they observe, and then exploring how the plants and small animals in this habitat survive together. Students also have the chance to look at photographs of "mystery" animal body parts (e.g., mouths, feet, and tails) and write captions describing how this body part might help an animal survive. In these ways, students are asking authentic questions and constructing their own answers (building knowledge!) in scaffolded and structured ways.

5. Organize each instructional cycle around a big idea or question to support the goal of deep learning.

We've talked a lot about the "meat" and the "bones" of the knowledge-building instructional cycle, and now we turn to the "connective tissue": An effective instructional cycle depends upon rich content, in the form of a big idea, for instructional organization and student inquiry. This element is our primary focus in the next chapter, but it is worth foreshadowing here because this is *how* the knowledge building happens. Without a big idea, we don't get to the knowledge building. That is, although each cycle will follow a similar developmental sequence of core learning tasks that involve reading, dialogue, and writing, the focus of the content learning changes from cycle to cycle. By delving into one big idea or question throughout the instructional cycle, you are setting up your students to engage in the process of deep learning. In the next chapter, we talk about how to select big ideas and questions to guide each instructional cycle.

What does this look like in Ms. Parkin's classroom?

Recall that right now, Ms. Parkin and her students are studying a big idea based in the life sciences: how animals survive in their environments. Their previous cycle was grounded in a social studies topic: how individuals and communities overcome obstacles. In Chapter 5, we look into how to choose big ideas like these and how to ground this content-based instruction in the reading and discussion of engaging texts.

PROTOCOLS FOR PLANNING AND REFLECTION

Planning My Own Knowledge-Building Cycle

Developmental Sequence	Core Learning Tasks	How Might I Adjust the Cognitive and Linguistic Demands?
Introducing Content and Engaging Students Around It		Early scaffolding: Later challenge:
Integrating What's Known with What's New		Early scaffolding: Later challenge:
Analyzing Word Forms, Meanings, and Uses (see Chapter 7 for ideas)		Early scaffolding: Later challenge:
Expanding Contexts and Applying Learning		Early scaffolding: Later challenge:
Extending What's Known to Produce a Message (see Chapter 8 for ideas)		Early scaffolding: Later challenge:

Self-Study: Is My Cycle a *Knowledge-Building* Cycle?

- Goes for depth
  - ☐ varied opportunities to study the big idea
  - ☐ varied opportunities to encounter and use target words
- Accommodates the process of knowledge and language development
  - ☐ sequence spanning at least 2 weeks
  - ☐ opportunities to talk through ideas, experiment with language, and engage in the process of trial and error
- Involves lots of opportunities for interaction
  - ☐ multiple, meaningful opportunities for content-focused, back-and-forth conversations
- Involves varied instructional methods
  - ☐ direct and explicit
  - ☐ inquiry-based
- Targets the different components of meaning-based literacy competencies
  - ☐ reading
  - ☐ writing
  - ☐ speaking and listening
- Incorporates varied instructional groupings
  - ☐ independent
  - ☐ pairs
  - ☐ small group
  - ☐ whole group

Develop Academic Content Knowledge by Studying Big Ideas

Her students left for the day, but Ms. Parkin still has company while she cleans up and arranges materials for tomorrow's centers. Jennifer O'Connor, a first-grade teacher at the school, sits at Ms. Parkin's lima bean–shaped table, cutting out word families for her own classroom's word sort center, eager to discuss the training they had both attended that morning. Jennifer lets out a frustrated sigh, "It's just that, we were at the training to talk about literacy instruction with English learners, not science or social studies instruction."

Ms. Parkin nods empathetically at her colleague and friend. Ms. O'Connor continues, "My literacy units focus on building good reading habits, on characters, story structure, and learning foundational skills. If I started making my units about science and social studies, when would I get my literacy goals accomplished?" Ms. Parkin remembers feeling that way herself several years back, when she too thought about reading and writing instruction as being largely about spelling words, comprehension strategies, and reading children's literature. She brings Camilla's portfolio with her—a former student of Ms. O'Connor's—and joins her friend at the table.

"I know what you mean. It's definitely a different way of thinking about literacy instruction, but I'm now certain that we can actually better teach those literacy skills and competencies while we're studying a complex topic, like one from science or social studies." Ms. Parkin opens up Camilla's folder, turning to a writing sample about Ruby, a character in *Ruby's Wish*, the touchstone text as part of their unit on overcoming obstacles. The writing sample explains how in that period of Chinese history, girls did not have the same learning opportunities as boys, but Ruby was determined not to let that get in the way of developing her reading and writing skills.

Ms. Parkin explains, "I know it's hard to imagine a shift toward more content, especially in first grade when there are so many skills to be mastered. But where I landed in the last few years is that content knowledge is literacy; we can't really separate them when we design our instruction. Even with foundational reading and writing skills, the knowledge doesn't really just 'develop.'"

Jennifer O'Connor nods, still scanning Camilla's description of Ruby. Ms. Parkin continues, "And what I still notice today is that my students are reading the words on the page and can answer basic comprehension questions, but when we really dig into content during a discussion or I look closely at their writing, they are still struggling with complex ideas and their language needs to be more academic. So, now I'm trying to organize my instruction around that." Jennifer looks up from Camilla's folder, furrowing her brow. "Yes, it's mostly the same for me. My students are learning their letters and sounds and developing phonics skills, but it's the content and ideas in the books that seems to trip many of them up."

There's no two ways about it: In a knowledge-building approach to literacy instruction, the content that focuses the learning for English learners (ELs), and the texts that act as touchstones for this study, are the cornerstone. As discussed in Chapters 3 and 4, a knowledge-building approach is framed and organized by an instructional cycle that follows a regular sequence of core learning tasks. While this routine is held constant, the academic content—the learning focus—changes from cycle to cycle, and each cycle revolves around a big idea. This sustained content focus is what makes the instructional cycle shine. As Ms. Parkin explained to Ms. O'Connor, the big idea under study is really a crucial platform for advancing each EL's knowledge, and therefore, literacy development. Here, we discuss the rationale behind focusing each cycle on a big idea. By *big idea*, we mean a multifaceted, academic topic with significant potential for student engagement. We also dig into why it's best to ground knowledge-building in a touchstone text. A *touchstone text* is a conceptually complex, accessible, and engaging text that features the big idea, acting as a springboard for learning and discussion throughout the cycle. Next, we provide important criteria for the selection of big ideas and their corresponding touchstone texts.

Why Study Big Ideas?

We weave a big idea throughout each knowledge-building cycle because, as we know from the instructional principles discussed in Chapter 3, a knowledge-building approach to reading instruction focuses on depth and process around learning. Each day, ELs engage with the same overarching topic, and with each successive learning opportunity, they have the chance to reconcile initial misunderstandings, consider this increasingly familiar topic in new ways, and approach the subject from different angles. Ultimately, after the longer-term investigation into this idea, ELs and their classroom peers are set up to generate their own message, theory, or argument about the topic.

As mentioned, text plays an important role in this knowledge-building approach. Each cycle is grounded in a touchstone text: a conceptually rich, accessible, and engaging text that features the big idea. Most often, we introduce the big idea and kick off the cycle through an interactive reading of the touchstone text, and then we come back to this text throughout the cycle, using it as a platform for conversation and learning. Each cycle is further punctuated by the reading of thematically related texts of all kinds: content-rich trade books, engaging magazine and Web-based articles, and leveled readers that are matched to children's particular skill levels, to name a few. Why use the interactive reading of texts as a tool for building content knowledge? Well, for one, when we engage our ELs and their peers in scaffolded, interactive readings of thematically related, varied texts, we are building collective understanding around the big idea that is the focus of study for the duration of the instructional cycle (Shanahan et al. 2010). The texts act as authentic contexts for encountering and engaging with the potentially unfamiliar words and novel concepts that are woven throughout the cycle (Beck and McKeown 2007). What's more, by using texts as a platform for content learning, we are giving ELs the very opportunity they need to try, practice, and experience "reading to learn"—something they will be expected to do throughout their schooling years (Moss 2005).

What Makes a Big Idea *Big*?

When selecting a topic for study throughout the knowledge-building cycle, the key is to ensure it's *big* enough to come back to again and again—that it enables ELs to study it from different perspectives and look at it from many different angles, all of which matters not just for learning but also for engagement. If it's not *big*, we won't get to the deep learning we intend, and we surely won't repeatedly engage our students in ways that keeps them active, and interactive, compromising our ability to support their deep knowledge building. But begs the question: What makes a big idea *big*? Figure 5.1 outlines what makes an idea a big one—what they are and what they are not.

Big Ideas Are . . .	Big Ideas Are Not . . .
▪ Multifaceted *What do we mean by* multifaceted? Big ideas are conceptually abstract and lend themselves to discussions around questions without one clear answer. Your students wouldn't just learn the topics related to these ideas in one shot but, instead, would need time and multiple, diverse, meaningful encounters to understand them deeply. *Multifaceted Idea: Forces That Make Things Move* There are lots of ways that objects move, different forces that move them, and many variables that influence changes in motion. Learning how, why, and what conditions influence changes in motion requires asking questions, observing evidence, and planning and carrying out investigations—not to mention learning from books read aloud and independently. Texts about construction, sports, outer space, weather, machines, and transportation all lend themselves to discussing forces and motion.	**▪ Straightforward** *What do we mean by* straightforward? Straightforward ideas are conceptually undemanding, with a clear and easy-to-understand explanation. Your students could grasp straightforward ideas with instruction provided through one or two lessons. *Straightforward Idea: Cause and Effect* Although some causes and their effects are conceptually abstract (like the forces that influence changes in motions), this common informational text structure, in of and itself, isn't multifaceted enough to design an entire instructional cycle around.
▪ Content-Based *What do we mean by* content-based? These ideas can often be explored through science, engineering, social studies, and the arts. Students are likely to return to aspects of these ideas throughout their schooling and life experiences. Beginning to build their knowledge and thinking around these topics now will support their learning for years to come. *Content-Based Idea: Forces That Make Things Move* Building knowledge of the physical sciences, including fundamental ideas about matter, energy, and motion, is something that can (and should!) be done from the earliest grades to the latest. Whether this rigorous, content-based big idea is studied in kindergarten (involving the investigation of gravity through marble painting) or in fourth grade (involving experimentation using static electricity), studying forces and motion across the grades prepares ELs for long-term learning and engagement with physics.	**▪ Strategy- or Skills-Based** *What do we mean by* strategy- or skills-based? ELs, like all learners, need to learn foundational literacy skills, the strategies associated with reading, and the structures associated with texts—in other words, the nuts and bolts of literacy. But, although these strategies and skills are important, they are not big ideas. In the knowledge-building classroom, literacy skills, reading strategies, and text types are learned within a content-based cycle, but they are not the drivers of that content. *Strategy-Based Idea: Cause and Effect* Organizing an instructional cycle around reading different texts that feature causes and effects, filling out cause-and-effect graphic organizers, predicting what an effect will be, and inferring the causes of particular results would certainly build ELs' competence around this text structure and related reading strategies, but these practices, alone, would not build their meaning-based literacy competencies. It is meaning-based literacy competencies that present the largest source of difficulty for most ELs.

continues

Figure 5.1 Big Ideas: What They Are and What They Are Not

continued

Big Ideas Are . . .	Big Ideas Are Not . . .
▪ Engaging *What do we mean by* engaging? These ideas tap into students' desires to be part of, and understand, the many worlds beyond school (Duke et al. 2012). These ideas are relevant to ELs' interests and experiences, but that's not all: They provide ELs with the opportunity to experience the excitement that accompanies beginning to understand something bigger than themselves (Duke et al. 2012). *Engaging Idea: Forces That Make Things Move* Forces and motion are all around us. In some classrooms, the study of forces and motion might begin by observing and drawing about how things move outdoors and then progress to classroom investigations using objects and simple machines that resemble playground equipment and toys, like balances, ramps, and spheres. These investigations can serve to bring texts featuring Newton's laws to life, helping students to move between the here and now and the abstract.	**▪ Just About "Doing School"** *What do we mean by* just about "doing school"? It would take a (stilted) leap to connect these to students' daily lives or to thought-provoking social and scientific issues. When students study these ideas, their main motivating factor is often doing well on the end-of-unit test or satisfying their teacher: There are few other worthwhile reasons to spend many days engaging with this content (Duke et al. 2012). *Just About "Doing School" Idea: Cause and Effect* Requiring students to generate cause-and-effect essays or reports is usually much more about doing school than about conveying information about the natural or social world to someone who wants or needs information. Similarly, reading a set of unrelated texts, all with the goal of determining causes and effects, has less to do with any authentic reason for reading, and instead, more to do with assignment completion.

Using the Dos and Don'ts of Big Ideas and Questions
Some More Examples and Nonexamples

Multifaceted, Content-Based, and Engaging	Straightforward, Strategy- or Skills-Based, and Just About "Doing School"
1. Forces That Make Things Move 2. How Relationships Influence Who We Are 3. How the Seasons Influence Living Things 4. How Regions of the United States Contribute to Our Union 5. Effecting Change in Our School 6. The Role of Poetry in Social Movements	1. Cause and Effect 2. Valentine's Day 3. What You Did on Your Summer Vacation 4. The Fifty States 5. Persuasive Essays 6. Different Types of Poems

What does this look like in Ms. Parkin's classroom?

As you might recall from earlier chapters, Ms. Parkin and her students are currently studying how animals survive in their environments. Throughout this cycle, Ms. Parkin guides her students as they learn why certain behaviors or physical adaptations benefit an organism's survival; build an understanding of the relationship between an organism's habitat and its adaptations; and gain insights into how changes in an animal's habitat will influence how well suited its adaptations are for its survival. What makes this big idea a big one (Figure 5.2)?

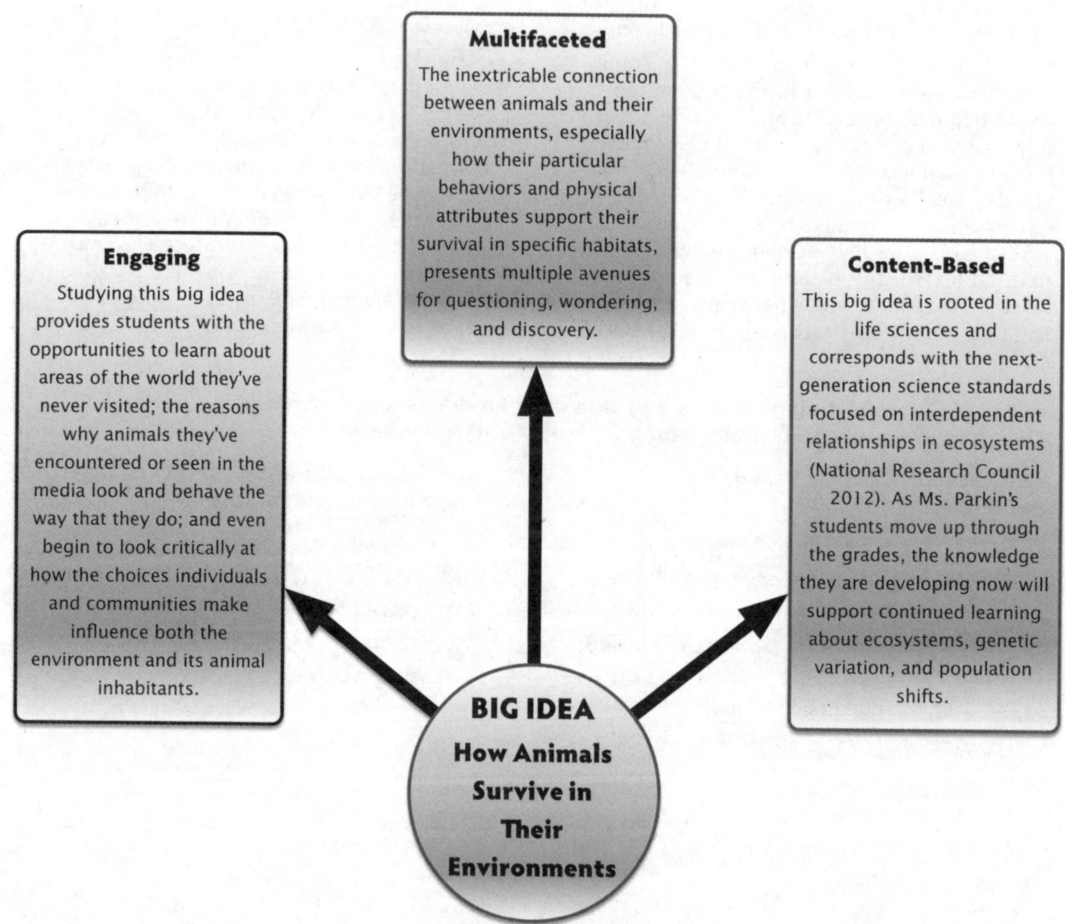

Multifaceted
The inextricable connection between animals and their environments, especially how their particular behaviors and physical attributes support their survival in specific habitats, presents multiple avenues for questioning, wondering, and discovery.
Engaging
Studying this big idea provides students with the opportunities to learn about areas of the world they've never visited; the reasons why animals they've encountered or seen in the media look and behave the way that they do; and even begin to look critically at how the choices individuals and communities make influence both the environment and its animal inhabitants.
Content-Based
This big idea is rooted in the life sciences and corresponds with the next-generation science standards focused on interdependent relationships in ecosystems (National Research Council 2012). As Ms. Parkin's students move up through the grades, the knowledge they are developing now will support continued learning about ecosystems, genetic variation, and population shifts.
BIG IDEA
How Animals Survive in Their Environments

Figure 5.2 What makes Ms. Parkin's big idea a *big* one?

How Do I Choose Touchstone Texts?

Again and again, teachers come to us with the same concern: How do I choose texts that will be really effective within this kind of knowledge-building instructional cycle but will also support my ELs, many of whom are struggling to read for meaning? It's a good and important question. Many teachers put significant time into finding texts with strong potential for learning and engagement, often spending hours browsing through stacks, bins, and shelves. After all, texts read aloud need to satisfy a number of criteria: be well written; have potential for being absorbing; have strong literary, scientific, or historical merit; be tailored for the purpose of instruction; be tailored to student needs; and so on. These teachers know that quality texts are foundational for building knowledge and spurring content-rich classroom conversations, so they wade through their school or public library, hoping the perfect texts will reveal themselves. Without guidelines for selecting texts—guidelines designed for the knowledge-building classroom—this process can be inefficient, too time-consuming, and, in the end, hit or miss. Here, we present several recommendations to steer your text selection process. We focus specifically on selecting the touchstone text for each cycle.

These recommendations are based on those outlined in articles and guides synthesizing research findings (Baker et al. 2014; Moss 2005; Saul and Dieckman 2005; Shanahan et al. 2010; Wisconsin Department of Public Education 2013) and articles describing text selection criteria for interventions conducted with linguistically diverse populations (Hickman, Pollard-Durodola, and Vaughn 2004; Lesaux, Kieffer et al. 2010; Lesaux, Harris, and Sloane 2012). We also referred to the criteria used by book award committees focused on content-based literature and texts. Specifically, in collaboration with the Children's Book Council (CBC), the National Science Teachers Association (NSTA) generates an annual list of Outstanding Science Trade Books, and the National Council on Social Studies (NCSS) generates an analogous list of Notable Social Studies Trade Books for Young People.

Interested in perusing the annually generated lists of Outstanding Science Trade Books and Notable Social Studies Trade Books for Young People? Find the titles, authors, and summaries of these high-quality, content-based texts at:

www.cbcbooks.org/outstanding-science
www.cbcbooks.org/notable-social-studies

What *type* of texts should I choose?

When choosing touchstone texts for knowledge-building literacy instruction, we want to be sure that the texts we choose will support our purpose: promoting deep thinking, discussion, and learning around the instructional cycle's big idea. Because the cycle's big idea should be content-based, we have found informational texts to be particularly well suited for this kind of teaching (Baker et al. 2014). Bear in mind, though, that "informational text" represents a very broad category.

For example, informational text (or "informative/explanatory") may include different genres, such as literary nonfiction and historical, scientific, and technical texts—all of which have as their primary purpose to convey information about the natural and social world, whether by describing how to do something or to persuade the reader (Common Core State Standards [CCSS] Initiative 2010; Duke et al. 2012; National Assessment Governing Board 2012). And so, within cycles, and especially across cycles, we want to be sure that ELs engage with an array of text types, thereby preparing them to read, understand, learn from, and generate a multiplicity of texts (Moss 2005). So, touchstone texts will often be trade books about science, engineering, history, social issues, or the arts but also magazine or newspaper articles, letters to the editor, op-ed columns, informative or provocative website entries, or speeches (Baker et al. 2014). Then, to build from each touchstone text, a knowledge-building cycle can include the reading of thematically relevant informational texts: from how-to books and reference guides to essays and biographies, timelines, graphs, and charts—lots can (and should) be learned from texts of all kinds (Duke et al. 2012; Moss 2005; Shanahan et al. 2010).

Although we can't overstate the importance of using informational texts in the knowledge-building classroom, it is inaccurate to assume that a singular text type can meet all of the knowledge-building needs of our ELs. We would be remiss if we did not call attention to the place of literary texts in the knowledge-building classroom—even if they're not our touchstone texts. In fact, if we are to support ELs to draw on a variety of perspectives, the reading of relevant children's literature is also highly recommended. For example, early in the school year, you might decide to focus a knowledge-building cycle on how we learn and grow, shedding light on how making and learning from mistakes helps our brains develop. Your touchstone text would likely be an informational book, like *Your Fantastic Elastic Brain* by Joann Deak (also available in Spanish), but it would also make good sense to layer on the reading of children's literature featuring characters who work through obstacles large and small, like *Whistle for Willie* by Ezra Jack Keats, *The Very Clumsy Click Beetle* by Eric Carle, and even the classic,

When it comes to finding trade books that can be used as a platform for building literacy and social-emotional skills simultaneously, the Center on Social Emotional Foundations for Early Learning is a great resource: http://csefel.vanderbilt.edu

The Little Engine That Could, by Watty Piper. In fact, when it comes to building children's social-emotional skills, such as perseverance, perspective-taking, tolerance, and emotional awareness, children's literature is a very good tool.

How long should the text be?

Ideally, the touchstone text for the knowledge-building cycle should be relatively brief (Baker et al. 2014). Short texts are easier to reread and revisit and are particularly amenable to deep exploration. They can also reduce the feeling of being overwhelmed that some ELs experience when listening to a long piece of text (Kelley et al. 2010).

At the same time, we understand that there could be lengthy, full books or articles you select as part of knowledge-building cycles that are long. If you select one of these for the touchstone text, then a lot of the knowledge-building instruction should focus on a key segment of the text—it may be the opening, it may be a specific section, or it may be a few pages that make good sense for deeper study. Of course, you will often want to read the full text, but bear in mind that your *knowledge-building* instructional activities (different from those to build reading stamina or promote the shared pleasure of reading a text uninterrupted, etc.) should focus on the key segment. For example, in a first-grade classroom, a book might be separated into a passage of 200–250 words for one purpose and a different passage for another instructional purpose (Hickman, Pollard-Durodola, and Vaughn 2004).

Although reading, discussing, and studying novels is certainly valuable for ELs' knowledge and literacy development, novels do not typically make for good touchstone texts. Instead, we view a function of the knowledge-building cycle as being to support students to be proficient and engaged with novels. For example, after two knowledge-building cycles, one focused on rights and responsibilities and the other on the ethical treatment of animals, an upper-elementary classroom might read *Shiloh*, by Phyllis Reynolds Naylor, analyzing the ways in which these themes are portrayed in the novel.

How many touchstone texts should I have for each cycle?

We recommend that each knowledge-building cycle lasts two to four weeks and is organized around one big idea. Each of these cycles is grounded in one touchstone text: a text that brings the big idea, or a key facet of this big idea, to life. Although the cycle is punctuated by the readings of multiple, diverse, thematically related texts, the single touchstone text plays a special role, both because of its depth and complexity, and, because of its use as a reference point throughout the cycle.

In some cases, each cycle will feature a new big idea and corresponding touchstone text. In others, you might link two or three knowledge-building cycles, creating a larger unit of study. That is, you can organize a set of cycles around a common big idea. In these cases, each cycle is grounded in a touchstone text that illustrates a facet of the overarching big idea.

For example, you might have a larger unit on the big idea, contributing to our community. The first knowledge-building cycle could focus on how it feels when we give to others. The touchstone text for this cycle might be *Sequoyah* by James Rumford or *The Birthday Swap* by Loretta Lopez. Then, the subsequent cycle might extend out to examine various ways in which individuals serve their community. This second knowledge-building cycle in this larger unit could use a magazine article about the role of community service in diverse communities and nations.

What reading level should the text be?

Choose touchstone texts at grade level for listening comprehension (Baker et al. 2014; Hickman, Pollard-Durodola, and Vaughn 2004; Lesaux, Kieffer et al. 2010; Lesaux, Harris, and Sloane 2012; Shanahan et al. 2010). This is often well above students' independent reading levels! We recognize that some of your ELs may not be able to deeply comprehend this reading material if asked to read independently or even with some scaffolding in the initial stage of working with the text. That's okay. Remember, with this approach to literacy instruction, we spend more time on specific topics and texts and provide significant, targeted support for word learning and comprehension. The important job we face in taking this approach is that of scaffolding instruction so that ELs are able to access the language of the text, grapple with the text's multifaceted topic, and understand new and challenging words.

What content should I look for?

Okay, this is a big one. First and foremost, your touchstone text should feature content that is relevant to the cycle's big idea. But beyond relevance, there are at least three content criteria to keep in mind when selecting touchstone texts for knowledge-building instruction. Touchstone texts should be complex, accurate, and discussion-worthy.

1. **Complex.** The touchstone text should provide sufficient detail and examples; use varied word choice and sentence structure; and, in many cases, include graphic features, such as illustrations, photographs, graphs, charts, diagrams, maps, or time lines, that complement and enhance the information provided linguistically (Saul and Dieckman 2005; Shanahan et al. 2010).
2. **Accurate.** The touchstone text should feature accurate and up-to-date information, clearly distinguish between theory and fact, and avoid oversimplifying facts to the point that they are misleading (National Science Teachers Association 2014; Saul and Dieckman 2005). At the same time, when you dig deep into it, it's hard to avoid the shades of gray that are inherent in accuracy and truth ("accuracy" is a big idea in and of itself!). Particularly when it comes to history, but even aspects of science, it is impossible to choose a text that isn't written from a particular perspective. So, it is important that students begin to learn to note *whose* truth a particular text is telling—and this type of approach will give you more opportunities to talk with students about it.
3. **Discussion-worthy.** The touchstone text should be useful for getting a conversation started. Texts that emphasize human relations, feature a character who faces a real-world problem, present substantial content, or raise a complex dilemma are often good choices for promoting discussion (National Council for the Social Studies 2013; Shanahan et al. 2010).

These three criteria should guide the selection of a cycle's touchstone text but can also inform your thinking when creating a set of thematically related texts that will complement your touchstone text or when thinking through how the touchstone texts used over the course of several knowledge-building cycles might fit together. When thinking about groups or sets of texts, however, there is a fourth criterion to consider: *diversity*. When contemplating a set of texts to be read over time, it is important to ensure that, together, they represent diverse ways of viewing and thinking about the many worlds beyond school. Each text might feature a fresh slant on a topic or real-world dilemma; present the perspective or experience of a different group, by culture, gender, or age, for example; take place in a different setting or geographical location; and/or provide elaborative details on a specific element of the topic (National Council for the Social Studies 2013; Saul and Dieckman 2005; Shanahan et al. 2010). The CCSS demonstrate a point of view on this idea of reading thematically related texts. Specifically, in the section titled "Staying on Topic Within a Grade and Across Grades," the importance of reading and discussing multiple, diverse texts that relate to a single topic is underscored, with the goal of providing opportunities for students to build depth of understanding (CCSS Initiative 2010, 33).

What vocabulary should I look for?

The words you choose for study in the knowledge-building cycle should be drawn from the touchstone text. So, you want to be sure that the text contains high-utility academic words (Baker et al. 2014). Academic words are common to school books but are much less common in conversation. These words are usually kind of meaty—a little complex, a little hard to explain, maybe some multiple meanings—and they are words that are useful when discussing and writing about the cycle's big idea. Encountering these words in texts, and building depth of knowledge around the concepts that these words represent, will support ELs' learning now, but also especially later. The very good news is this: When you choose a complex, discussion-worthy text that illustrates the cycle's big idea, having high-utility academic words is almost inevitable. Once in a while, there will be a particular academic word that is *not* used in your touchstone text but is highly conceptually related to the cycle's big idea and will greatly facilitate students' talking and writing about the content under study. In these cases, the vast majority of the academic words studied in the cycle will be drawn from the touchstone text, but one or two key concepts that would make excellent target words are not. See Chapter 6 for more about how to select vocabulary words for study.

But what about the rest of the texts in the cycle's set? Should they all feature the same academic words? Well, in the best-case scenario, this corpus of texts, together, would provide multiple encounters with the cycle's target words. But because the full instructional cycle will weave opportunities to talk and write with the target words throughout—opportunities that go beyond listening to them in texts. We don't think that your only focus should be on searching for sets of texts that all feature the same set of words. On the contrary, it would be particularly beneficial for ELs to engage with thematically related texts that feature varied, rich, word choice and sentence structure (Baker et al. 2014; Shanahan et al. 2010).

How and where do leveled readers fit into a knowledge-building approach?

A leveled book collection, organized carefully around gradients of difficulty, is a go-to resource for many elementary school teachers. In classrooms all over, teachers select books from these sets, using them with guided reading groups and filling students' independent reading bins or bags with "just-right" books. Decodable books—those written to provide readers with practice applying a particular set of sound–letter relations—are also often used in this way.

As important as these books may be for developing code-based foundational skills (see Chapter 1 for a full description of code-based and meaning-based skills), given the nature of the way we select and use them, they do not play a central role in the knowledge-building approach to literacy instruction. This approach necessarily demands complex content and ideas, and often content is not what's driving our selection of these texts or how we use them. For example, the leveled reader is typically selected using a running record, based on how well it matches students' capacities with accurate and efficient word reading. Yes, as part of this code-based work we almost always ask students to tell us what the guided-reading book was about and we invariably check for understanding. But if our primary goal were building knowledge about complex ideas and developing meaning-making skills, then we'd choose different texts for these very important small-group learning opportunities. And if these leveled readers are the only texts that our readers are exposed to, then we worry about lack of opportunities to engage with rich content.

For these reasons, leveled readers and decodable books are not one of our touchstone texts—they just aren't designed to serve as a platform for ongoing, content-rich classroom conversations. Still, leveled readers and decodable books have a role to play in literacy instruction, and it would be a good idea if they were thematically related to the unit of study. In fact, guided reading groups could potentially serve as an opportunity to build students' understanding of the language and content under focus during a knowledge-building cycle. Importantly then, if we're thinking about knowledge building in our guided reading groups, at least as much as we're thinking about code-based skill development, in lots of cases we're going to need to start choosing more complex leveled readers and organizing lessons differently.

What does this look like in Ms. Parkin's classroom?

For her instructional cycle focused on the big idea of how animals survive in their environments, Ms. Parkin chose the book *Why Do Tigers Have Stripes?* by Mike Unwin, as the cycle's touchstone text. Let's take a look at the aspects of this text that led Ms. Parkin to select it (Figure 5.3).

Studying Big Ideas and Big Words to Cultivate Knowledge in the Linguistically Diverse Classroom

At this point, you are well on your way to making the shift to knowledge-building literacy instruction. As Ms. O'Connor—the first-grade teacher down the hall from Ms. Parkin—is learning, when we consistently and deliberately organize instruction around the deep learning of complex, content-based, and engaging topics, our classrooms become places where ELs accumulate knowledge on an ongoing basis. And by grounding these content-based learning opportunities in complex and discussion-worthy texts, we are supporting ELs to develop the foundation they need to access and generate a range of texts now and as they grow up—the advanced literacy skills needed for today's society.

So, when designing literacy instruction using this knowledge-building approach as an overarching framework and with a cycle, big idea, and corresponding touchstone text in place, what comes next in instructional planning? Well, just as each knowledge-building cycle requires a platform (i.e., a big idea) for developing ELs' academic content knowledge, each cycle also requires a parallel platform for more squarely focusing on ELs' academic language development. For this, we turn to academic words: abstract vocabulary terms that are common to school texts and talk and are particularly useful for communicating and thinking about disciplinary content (Nagy and Townsend 2012). In Chapter 6, we discuss why cultivating deep understanding of academic words matters for ELs and how to select those words that will actually strengthen the study of your knowledge-building cycle's big idea and support comprehension of the cycle's touchstone text.

Features of Touchstone Texts	***Why Do Tigers Have Stripes?* by Mike Unwin**
Informational text related to the cycle's big idea	This informational text acts as a platform for promoting deep thinking, discussion, and learning about the cycle's big idea. This book focuses on the role that color plays in animal survival, describing how colors can conceal or warn, attract or repel, disguise or reveal. As different animals and their color-related adaptations are described, the ways in which these adaptations are linked to the animal's environment are also highlighted.
Relatively brief	The book is twenty-three pages (~100–150 word on each page). The book is divided into sections, each of which is featured on a two-page spread. These sections present high-level summaries of the different ways that animals use color to survive as well as examples of these adaptation types.
On grade level	This text could be considered a grade-level text: Ms. Parkin can read this book aloud to her third graders; with the right scaffolding, they can comprehend, learn from, and discuss it.
Complex, accurate, and discussion-worthy content	▪ This text describes the various ways in which coloration supports animal's survival (e.g., surprises, keep-away colors, signals) as well as several examples of each. These examples are complemented by multiple, captioned illustrations. ▪ The information provided in this book represents accurate and up-to-date information. Although some points are simplified, they are not misleading or inaccurate (e.g., the book does not always include the scientific terms for the concepts described, such as mimicry and bioluminescence, but these concepts are described accurately). ▪ The substantial content presented in this book bodes well for getting conversations started and keeping them going. Discussions might revolve around the different functions colors play in animal survival, the relationship between animal colors and the other organisms in their environments, or how the animals' use of colors in this book compare and contrast to the ways in which humans use color (e.g., to blend in, stand out, to attract).
Features academic vocabulary	This text includes a portion of words that are *academic* in nature: words that are useful for talking about academic content and represent abstract concepts (e.g., *adaptation, attract, disguise, environment, patterns, recognize, reflect, shadow, surface, survive*).

Figure 5.3 Ms. Parkin's Touchstone Text

PROTOCOLS FOR PLANNING AND REFLECTION

Big Ideas and Touchstone Texts: Selection Guidelines

Potential Big Idea: ______________________________

Is This Idea a *Big* One?	Notes to Self
Multifaceted ☐ Conceptually abstract ☐ Amenable to discussions around questions without clear answers ☐ Requires study over time for deep understanding (e.g., multiple, diverse, meaningful encounters)	
Content-Based ☐ Rooted in science, social studies, and/or the arts ☐ Relates to topics and ideas that will support academic learning as students move up through the grades	
Potential for Engagement ☐ Provides an opportunity to become interested and engaged in a new idea or concept	

Potential Text: ______________________________

Does This Text Meet the Criteria for a Knowledge-Building Touchstone Text?	**Notes to Self**
☐ Informational text related to the cycle's big idea	
☐ Relatively brief, to serve as a platform for study	
☐ On grade level (Think listening–comprehension level!)	
☐ Features academic vocabulary	
☐ Quality content	
☐ Complex	
☐ Accurate	
☐ Discussion-worthy	

Provide Consistency by Organizing Lessons Within a Cycle

Develop Academic Content Knowledge by Studying Big Ideas

Develop Academic Vocabulary Knowledge by Studying a Small Set of Words Deeply

Unlock Language by Developing Word-Learning Strategies

Extend Learning with Language Production Projects

Develop Academic Vocabulary Knowledge by Studying a Small Set of Words Deeply

A BALLGAME INSIDE EVERY BOOK?

Why Depth of Vocabulary Knowledge Matters

On a blustery summer day in Boston's Fenway Park, 40,000 fans watch a towering pop-up fall in a strange spiral as three Atlanta Braves dance below, gloves opened, attempting to catch it. The windblown ball drops to the ground near second base, prompting two ten-year-olds seated in the bleachers to react. One of them, Nathan, cheers and jumps up in delight. Several rows away, ten-year-old Isabella sits down dejectedly and sighs. Unlike Nathan, she knows the Red Sox batter is automatically out via the infield fly rule—and she's bothered that the Red Sox rally appears over.

It's been going this way since the ballgame began—same play, different reactions. In the third inning, the announcer informed the crowd that the Red Sox hit was ruled to have gone just to the left of Pesky's Pole. Isabella joined the fans who cheered for the home run. Nathan didn't get what all the fuss was about. Then in the sixth, when fans loudly applauded a Braves relief pitcher—long a local favorite when he played for Boston—Nathan sat quietly, unaware of why the opposing pitcher was given such a warm reception from the Boston fans. As the complexities of the competition continued to appear, Isabella felt her pulse quicken and ran through scenarios of what might happen next.

Nathan, meanwhile, felt his interest wane. Nathan and Isabella both stayed through to the end of ninth inning, but they walked out onto Lansdowne Street having had very different experiences because of what they "brought" to Fenway, their background knowledge about baseball and its vocabulary. (Adapted from Lesaux 2010)

What does watching baseball have to do with reading?

When someone goes to watch a baseball game, it's much the same as picking up a book to read. The value of each experience varies from person to person, even though the plays on the field and the words on the page don't differ. The ball game experience will be superficial or deep, broad or specific, depending upon your prior experiences. Everyone gets something from having gone to the ballpark, just as all readers get something from having read the book; without relevant background and vocabulary knowledge, though, the novice is at a disadvantage from the first inning or the first page.

When it comes to the ins and outs of baseball (no pun intended), Nathan gets the gist but requires many more opportunities to watch, learn, and play if he is going to experience the depth of understanding Isabella demonstrates. Similarly, many of today's English learners (ELs) enter our classrooms well beyond the beginning stages of English proficiency. But when it comes to the words and concepts that are most critical for long-term academic success, many ELs are operating somewhere between very shallow and deep knowledge. Recall from Chapter 3, there is a continuum of word knowledge, such that a learner has a particular "level" or "degree" of understanding, of which there are at least five: no knowledge; general sense; narrow, context-bound knowledge; enough knowledge to understand but not necessarily enough to recall and use it appropriately; and rich, decontextualized knowledge of the word's meaning, its relationship to other words, and metaphorical use (Beck, McKeown, and Kucan 2013, 11).

So what does all of this mean for our approach to literacy instruction? It is time to get very serious about providing ELs with significantly more opportunities to develop the sophisticated, abstract, academic vocabulary necessary to support reading, writing, and discussion of the academic topics studied in school (August and Shanahan 2006). As discussed in Chapter 2, *academic vocabulary* represents words that are used primarily in the academic content areas (science, history, geography, mathematics, literary analysis, etc.). These words are much more frequently used in discussions, essays, and articles in these disciplines than in everyday conversations and social settings. Typically, academic vocabulary is broken into two categories: *general academic* vocabulary and *content-specific* vocabulary (Baker et al. 2014).

- General academic vocabulary words, such as *environment*, *factor*, *exhibit*, *investigate*, *transition*, and *tangential*, are used in writing across many academic disciplines.
- Content-specific academic vocabulary words are unique to a particular academic discipline. Words such as *pi* and *commutative* are linked to mathematics; words like *diode* and *atom* are linked to physics.

In the sections that follow, we outline the reasons why studying a small set of academic words deeply is a crucial part of the knowledge-building classroom. We then describe how to select academic words for study in the context of a knowledge-building instructional cycle. To bring this selection process to life, we provide a window into each step undertaken by two teachers: Ms. Parkin, the third-grade teacher featured in the previous chapters and her colleague, Ms. Bruno, a fourth-grade teacher.

Why Study a Small Set of Words Deeply?

For students to comprehend and generate academic text and to participate in academic dialogue, they require a deep understanding of the words that we consider the bricks and mortar of academic language. When a learner has deep knowledge of a word, she has a rich understanding of what it means, how it relates to other words, and how it is useful in multiple contexts. Having this conceptual knowledge means that whether we are a reader or listener engaging in academic text and talk, we are full participants.

But because word knowledge exists in degrees, we need to be very concerned that many of our students—especially our ELs—are not reaching levels that are considered deep enough to support their reading comprehension. The most recent body of reading comprehension research conducted with linguistically diverse elementary school–age learners highlights the particular importance and the instructional challenge of building students' deep vocabulary knowledge. Although a large amount of literacy research conducted with ELs shows that vocabulary knowledge, generally, is a common source of reading difficulties (Lesaux et al. 2006), recent research confirms that the degree to which ELs have *deep* vocabulary knowledge is a large and significant predictor of their reading comprehension, often above and beyond their vocabulary size (Kieffer and Lesaux 2008, 2012; Leider et al. 2013; Proctor et al. 2009, 2012). This information matters greatly for how we think about promoting vocabulary development in our classrooms. The findings show that familiarity with a large number of words and a rich understanding of what these words mean are not one in the same. And the latter is a difference maker for ELs' literacy development—and therefore their school success. The story of Nathan and Isabella in the chapter's opening illustrates this point. That is, although both Nathan and Isabella might be familiar with general baseball terms like *bunt*, *strike zone*, and *triple play*, as well as Boston Red Sox–specific terms and concepts like *Pesky's Pole*, *Curse of the Bambino*, and *"Sweet Caroline,"* their depth of understanding of these words and concepts are vastly different. And in turn, what they experience during the ball game, and what they take away from it, also differs.

What does this mean for instruction in classrooms with ELs? First, because of the crucial nature of deep vocabulary knowledge for reading comprehension, we can no longer start with long lists of words, teach them through a series of memorization activities and independent worksheets, and then move on. Instead, we need to choose small sets of words for extensive study (Baker et al. 2014). Second, we cannot rely on wide reading to deepen word knowledge (Beck, McKeown, and Kucan 2013). So, although it may be the case that ELs in our classrooms need exposure to lots of words, when it comes to accomplishing our goal of teaching that results in advanced literacy skills, wide exposure and coverage alone simply won't cut it. Instead, it's time to build up ELs' knowledge by digging into concepts and the words used to represent them. In so doing, learners will have the chance to develop nuanced understandings of the conceptual relationships among academic words, the ways in which these words can be combined in context to create grammatically correct and meaningful sentences, and the ways in which words are made up of meaningful parts like roots, prefixes, and suffixes. Importantly, by going for depth on a small set of academic words, we are actually providing ELs and their peers with the knowledge and skills they need to most effectively take advantage of the many word-learning opportunities they will encounter down the line, thereby supporting them not only to have a sufficient vocabulary now but also to be better equipped to learn unfamiliar words they encounter down the road (this principle is sometimes referred to as "bootstrapping"). Ready to get started? Let's select vocabulary terms for study.

HOW TO RESPOND WHEN ADMINISTRATORS SAY YOU SHOULD BE TEACHING MORE WORDS

We've hopefully made it very clear that studying a small set of words deeply is a research-based, practical, and effective approach to developing ELs' vocabulary knowledge in ways that will translate to ongoing academic success. But we also know that having looked at achievement gaps, literacy levels, and just how much instructional ground there is to cover in a short time, not surprisingly, the response of some school administrators and district leaders is to push a "more is more approach." These individuals persist with the idea that teachers should cover long lists of words each week in an effort to close gaps and boost achievement more quickly. To help you act as an ambassador for the research indicating the importance of choosing small sets of words for extensive study (going for depth!), we've summarized points from this chapter and others. Use these talking points to support your conversations with well-intentioned but potentially misguided advocates for "more."

Studying a small set of word deeply is responsive to ELs' learning strengths and needs because:

1. **Many ELs have *some* understanding of a whole lot of words—but not enough depth for comprehension, academic speech, or writing.** When it comes to the words and concepts that are critical for academic success (e.g., academic words like *environment*, *investigate, transition*), many ELs have only very shallow knowledge. Teaching *more* words will not fix the problem of lack of command of the academic words needed for academic success.
2. **There is a strong relationship between ELs' depth of vocabulary knowledge and their reading comprehension.** Recent research indicates that the degree to which ELs have deep vocabulary knowledge is a large and significant predictor of their reading comprehension, often above and beyond the sheer size of their vocabulary.
3. **It is only with well-developed word-learning skills and deep word study that we begin to accumulate broad knowledge.** When we teach a small set of words deeply, our ELs are necessarily

studying a number of words around the target word—and when doing this, students develop metacognitive strategies (e.g., monitoring for meaning, problem-solving, information-seeking). These strategies are useful when the reader comes across a word she doesn't know—and especially important when the exposure to the new, unfamiliar word is under brief or independent conditions, such as during a read-aloud or while reading independently.

How Do I Choose Words for Study?

Although we can't possibly engage in deep study of all of the academic words that students need to learn, we can—and must!—choose our words wisely (Nagy and Hiebert 2011). Ultimately, in each knowledge-building cycle, you will deeply study roughly 5–10 words. The exact number of words will depend upon your students' age and grade level and the amount of time you are devoting to the knowledge-building instructional cycle. However, selecting more than ten words for intensive instruction is likely to be counterproductive. When vocabulary instruction focuses on teaching a large number of words in a day, or even a week, students develop only a shallow understanding of a word's meaning—and this meaning is only rarely retained and rarely useful for supporting reading comprehension. When we start with fewer words and devote more time to studying them, we support ELs as they learn the concepts and nuances associated with a given word. They have multiple chances to practice using words through writing, speaking, and listening learning tasks.

Here, we provide a three-step process for selecting words worth teaching. Each step is described and then represented on a tool we call a *Word Selection Matrix* (Figure 6.1). Using this matrix, list potential target words along the far left column (step 1), and then determine whether each word meets the criteria listed across the top rows (step 2). Based on these determinations, narrow down and finalize the list (step 3). We provide a full-size matrix in the Protocols for Planning and Reflection at the end of the chapter.

These steps and the corresponding Word Selection Matrix are applied to the text *Zoos Then and Now*. Ms. Parkin's colleague, Ms. Bruno, a fourth-grade teacher at her school, is using this article as the touchstone text for an instructional cycle focused on the ethical treatment of animals. After we see how Ms. Bruno moves through this word selection process, we also check back in with Ms. Parkin. We'll see how she uses these steps to select target words for her current cycle, focused on how animals survive in their environments. With these steps and examples at your fingertips, you'll be set to select academic words for study in your classroom.

Step 1: From the touchstone read-aloud text, identify a pool of potential academic words for teaching.

The words chosen for study in each knowledge-building cycle should be drawn from the touchstone text—the primary text used throughout the cycle (see Chapter 5). Why start with a touchstone text, rather than a list of academic words? As previously described, when we pull target academic words from a text that will be read, talked about, and analyzed in a highly interactive, collaborative manner, we are guaranteeing that our students will encounter these words authentically and in the context that's giving them trouble—the academic language of print. And because this text revolves around the cycle's *big* idea and is at your ELs' listening comprehension (rather than independent reading) level, the text will inevitably include the kinds of high-utility academic words that our learners need. As you might recall, *academic vocabulary* words appear throughout the curriculum and typically fall into two categories: *general academic* vocabulary and *content-specific* vocabulary (Baker et al. 2014). Taking a knowledge-building approach to literacy instruction means that we focus our instruction primarily on general academic vocabulary: words such as *evidence*, *community, and process*, used in writing across many academic disciplines.

Okay, let's start. First, as you read your touchstone text, note all the academic words that you spot, generating your pool for teaching. List these words along the far-left column of your Word Selection Matrix (Figure 6.1). That's step 1. We've got two examples for reference: Figure 6.2 shows the text that Ms. Bruno plans to read with her fourth graders; within it, her pool of potential target words for study are highlighted. You might find that you'd highlight many of the same words—or different ones. In Figure 6.3, we show you the pool of potential target words Ms. Parkin has identified from her touchstone text, along with some of her initial thoughts, and we discuss those further below.

	USEFULNESS					**COMPLEXITY**		
Potential Target Words	*For This Text*	*For This Big Idea*	*For Big Ideas to Come*	*Across Content Areas*	*In a Particular Content Area*	*Conceptually Abstract*	*Polysemous*	*Morphologically Challenging*

Figure 6.1 Word Selection Matrix

FROM THE TOUCHSTONE READ-ALOUD TEXT, IDENTIFY A POOL OF POTENTIAL ACADEMIC WORDS FOR TEACHING

Teacher: Ms. Bruno
Grade level: 4
Big Idea: Ethical Treatment of Animals
Touchstone Text: Zoos Then and Now

When you walk into a zoo today, the exhibits look different than they used to look years ago. Before the 1960s, zoos had cages with tile walls and floors. Now, animals in zoos live in more natural environments. For example, instead of enormous gorillas pacing back and forth in cramped cement areas, they play on soft grass and nap in trees. Before, large birds lived in small cages. Now, zoos have large exhibits where birds can stretch their wings and soar from tree to tree. According to zoo design expert Jon C. Coe, these changes often have a positive impact on animals' health and happiness.

Still, creating better living spaces is just one step toward improving the lives of animals that live in zoos. Even in exhibits that look like their natural environments, animals can become bored. According to Coe, an exhibit may look great, but it isn't doing much for the animal unless it also involves a choice of things to do all day. Animals need to be challenged with activities such as looking for food and exploring their surroundings. In fact, some research has shown that giving zoo animals more options and activities promotes good health and lowers the incidence of violent behavior. Today, several zoos have created living environments for their animals that involve the kinds of pursuits that Coe described. For instance, the orangutans at the National Zoo in Washington, DC can travel across the zoo on overhead ropes to visit friends.

Coe recommends more investigation into these types of zoo exhibits and their impact on animal health. With this new pursuit of creating more natural environments in zoo exhibits, he sees a happier and healthier future for many zoo animals.

Sample text adapted from "Designing Zoo Habitats That Promote Animal Well-Being" by R. Scott Nolen, posted November 2, 2002 in *JAVMA News* (December 1, 2002), www.avma.org.

Figure 6.2 Step 1 in Action

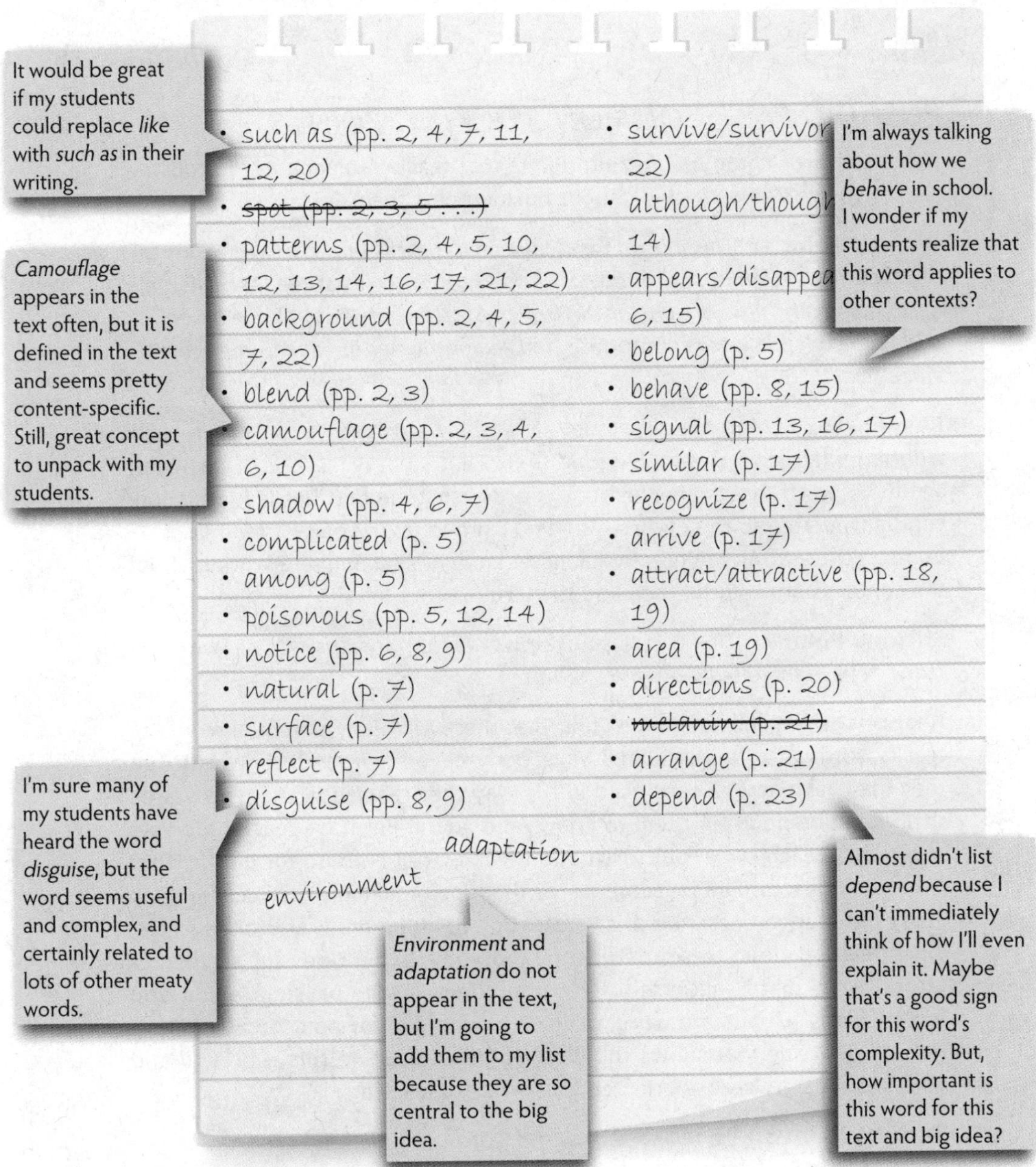

It would be great if my students could replace *like* with *such as* in their writing.
• such as (pp. 2, 4, 7, 11, 12, 20)
• ~~spot (pp. 2, 3, 5 . . .)~~
• patterns (pp. 2, 4, 5, 10, 12, 13, 14, 16, 17, 21, 22)
• background (pp. 2, 4, 5, 7, 22)
• blend (pp. 2, 3)
• camouflage (pp. 2, 3, 4, 6, 10)
• shadow (pp. 4, 6, 7)
• complicated (p. 5)
• among (p. 5)
• poisonous (pp. 5, 12, 14)
• notice (pp. 6, 8, 9)
• natural (p. 7)
• surface (p. 7)
• reflect (p. 7)
• disguise (pp. 8, 9)
• survive/survivor
22)
• although/though
14)
• appears/disappea
6, 15)
• belong (p. 5)
• behave (pp. 8, 15)
• signal (pp. 13, 16, 17)
• similar (p. 17)
• recognize (p. 17)
• arrive (p. 17)
• attract/attractive (pp. 18, 19)
• area (p. 19)
• directions (p. 20)
• ~~melanin (p. 21)~~
• arrange (p. 21)
• depend (p. 23)
adaptation
environment
Camouflage appears in the text often, but it is defined in the text and seems pretty content-specific. Still, great concept to unpack with my students.
I'm always talking about how we *behave* in school. I wonder if my students realize that this word applies to other contexts?
I'm sure many of my students have heard the word *disguise*, but the word seems useful and complex, and certainly related to lots of other meaty words.
Environment and *adaptation* do not appear in the text, but I'm going to add them to my list because they are so central to the big idea.
Almost didn't list *depend* because I can't immediately think of how I'll even explain it. Maybe that's a good sign for this word's complexity. But, how important is this word for this text and big idea?

Figure 6.3 Ms. Parkin's Pool of Potential Academic Words for Teaching

PUSHING PAST COMMON STICKING POINTS

There are three common sticking points that teachers encounter in this initial step. Here's how we think about pushing past them.

Sticking Point 1: *"There is an academic term that is incredibly relevant to the cycle I'm designing, but it doesn't appear in my touchstone text. My big idea is, literally, how regions of the United States contribute to our union, and the academic words* contribute *and* region *do not appear in my touchstone text."*

Response: The vast majority, if not all, of the words you study in each cycle will be pulled from the touchstone text. That said, if there is a particular academic word that is absent from your touchstone text but is highly conceptually related to the cycle's big idea, used in texts you will read later on in the cycle, and/or will greatly facilitate students' talking and writing about the content under study, then add the term to your list.

Sticking Point 2: *"This text has lots of words that my students need to learn—I've highlighted way more than ten."*

Response: You will sometimes find that there are many potential words to teach: words that your students have likely never heard before, words that they may have never heard used in the way they're used in the text, words that would be good for them to know, and so on. But if we teach long lists of words in each cycle, our instruction won't be able to go for depth. That being said, there might be some words that don't make the final cut for deep study but that you describe or call attention to along the way—for example, when reading aloud to your students and you reach a rare (not academic/target) word that is necessary for comprehending the passage. Here, you might briefly explain the word, provide a synonym, or point to an illustration on the page that shows the word (Kindle 2009). In this way, you and your students are always oriented toward word learning.

Sticking Point 3: *"I'm not sure if all the words I highlighted are truly 'academic.' Should I check them all against a particular list?"*

Response: It's tricky because although there are lists (e.g., Coxhead 2011; Marzano and Pickering 2005) and criteria (e.g., Beck, McKeown, and Kucan 2002) that begin to help us identify these words, the reality is that there is no exact boundary that dichotomizes academic and nonacademic words (Snow 2010). We recommend that you highlight all of the words that strike you as more common to school texts than to everyday communication, and move to step 2.

Sticking Point 4: *"I'm not sure how familiar my students are with the academic words in this text so I'm not sure which ones to highlight."*

Response: When it comes to choosing academic words for study, we are more concerned with the word's utility and complexity and less worried about ELs' specific degree of familiarity. Our goal is to increase students' depth of word knowledge, so choosing words with respect to students' degree of knowledge is less important than focusing on those that appear in text across content areas and curricula.

Step 2: Evaluate all potential academic words on two dimensions: usefulness and complexity.

Now that you have the text and a list of potential target words in front of you, it's time to begin to find out how these words stack up in two important ways: usefulness and complexity. The Word Selection Matrix lists these two dimensions across the top row and then enumerates the particular criteria that correspond with these broad organizing factors.

Usefulness

When choosing academic words for study, it's important to consider the degree to which each word is useful. By useful—or high-utility—we mean that studying these words will support learning now, but especially later. How do we know that deep knowledge of a word is, and will be, useful? There are at least five criteria to keep in mind. Useful words are:

- necessary for understanding the text in which it appears and so studying this word will scaffold ELs' comprehension of this text
- central to talking and writing about the big idea under study and so learning to use this word flexibly will support ELs' active engagement across the knowledge-building cycle
- connected to big ideas in past and future instructional cycles
- central to understanding, discussing, and writing across a variety of academic content areas (i.e., general academic vocabulary words like *contribute*, *dimension*, and *valid*)
- central to understanding, discussing, and writing in a particular academic content area (i.e., content-specific academic vocabulary words like *respiration*, *sediment*, and *crescendo*); some general academic words have content-specific meanings, like the words *area* and *factor*, which have precise meanings in math but are used more generally across content areas.

It bears mentioning here that the main reason general and content-specific academic vocabulary words are useful is because they will continue to be (frequently!) used in academic talk and text throughout ELs' schooling experiences. In fact, if you work in a school that's particularly vertically aligned, you could discuss useful words for study with teachers working in upper grade levels. Take a look at Figure 6.4 to see how Ms. Bruno decides on the usefulness of each potential words. There are always gray areas with this exercise, and of course, we're missing lots of context on Ms. Bruno's curriculum and yearlong plan, so you may or may not agree with her evaluation or see an obvious connection; the important piece here is that she is thoughtfully considering the criteria, weighing the relative usefulness of each word.

EVALUATE THE USEFULNESS OF POTENTIAL ACADEMIC WORDS

Teacher: Ms. Bruno

Grade Level: 4

Big Idea: Ethical Treatment of Animals

Touchstone Text: *Zoos Then and Now*

	USEFULNESS				
Potential Target Words	For This Text	For This Big Idea	For Big Ideas to Come	Across Content Areas	In a Particular Content Area
Exhibit	✓			✓	
Natural	✓	✓			✓
Environment	✓	✓	✓	✓	✓
Area				✓	✓
According to	✓			✓	
Design	✓		✓	✓	
Expert	✓	✓	✓	✓	
Impact	✓	✓	✓	✓	✓
Surroundings	✓		✓		
Promotes	✓	✓	✓	✓	
Incidence	✓	✓		✓	
Involve	✓		✓		
Pursuit	✓			✓	
Investigation			✓	✓	

continues

Figure 6.4A Step 2 in Action

EVALUATE THE COMPLEXITY OF POTENTIAL ACADEMIC WORDS

Teacher: Ms. Bruno

Grade Level: 4

Big Idea: Ethical Treatment of Animals

Touchstone Text: *Zoos Then and Now*

	COMPLEXITY		
Potential Target Words	Conceptually Abstract	Polysemous	Morphologically Challenging
Exhibit	✓	✓	✓
Natural	✓	✓	✓
Environment	✓	✓	✓
Area		✓	
According to		✓	
Design	✓	✓	✓
Expert		✓	
Impact	✓	✓	
Surroundings			
Promotes	✓	✓	✓
Incidence	✓		✓
Involve	✓	✓	✓
Pursuit		✓	
Investigation			✓

Figure 6.4B Step 2 in Action *(continued)*

Complexity

Complexity is the other dimension to consider. You want to choose words that are complex enough that they are unlikely to be learned from context or in passing but yet are central to making meaning from academic text. You might be surprised by how complex, opaque, and hard to explain some seemingly "common" words are and how some rare and seemingly "difficult" words are really not that complex at all—they can be learned relatively easily. What makes a word complex? Complex words tend to be characterized by one or more of the following features.

- **Conceptually abstract.** Complex words are not easily defined in the way concrete nouns, like *table* and *chair* (and even *cheetah* and *arboretum*), are and therefore require study and extended discussion to grasp the concepts they represent (e.g., *transform*, *community*, and *process*, as well as connective words and phrases like *although*, *consequently*, *in contrast*).
- **Polysemous.** They often have multiple, related meanings; when they are used in different contexts or in different subject areas, their meanings change somewhat. For example, the words *volume* and *remainder* could be encountered in a math or a social studies lesson, but these words would likely be used differently depending on these contexts.
- **Morphologically challenging.** By adding or taking away prefixes and/or suffixes, you can change the meaning or grammatical forms of these words (e.g., *transform*, *transformation*, *transformable*, *transformative*).

Just like she did for the usefulness dimension, as shown in Figure 6.4A, Ms. Bruno evaluates each of her potential target words on the complexity dimension: whether each is conceptually abstract, polysemous, and/or morphologically challenging (Figure 6.4B). For some words, she consulted an online dictionary, just to double-check whether or not certain words had other morphological forms or multiple meanings. Conceptual abstractness was a little less cut-and-dried, but she decided that her rule of thumb would be to check those that she didn't feel she could define for students quickly while providing an adequately rich explanation—not because she doesn't know the word, but because the word is hard to explain.

WANT MORE EXAMPLES OF ACADEMIC WORDS?

- Averil Coxhead (2011) developed an academic word list that includes the 570 most common general academic word families in college-level texts across four disciplines. Several websites post this list for free viewing, including Victoria University of Wellington's website www.victoria.ac.nz/lals/resources/academicwordlist/ (where Coxhead works).
- Robert Marzano and Debra Pickering (2005) developed domain-specific academic word lists (their book includes 7,923 vocabulary terms for eleven content areas, further divided by grade-level clusters). Adapted versions of these domain-specific lists are free to view online on the Wordlists page of the WordSift website (www.wordsift.com/wordlists), which is designed to support educators' academic vocabulary instruction, including target word selection.

Step 3: Finalize your list.

Now that you have completed the Word Choice Matrix, you will have a map illustrating the ways in which each potential word for teaching stacks up against the usefulness and complexity dimensions. In step 3, we use this information to help us narrow down and finalize the list. In part, narrowing down your list involves prioritizing individual words that meet multiple criteria, but we also want to think about how a collection of words will hang together as a set. For example, if you would like to do some morphology work, such as practice transforming words using the suffix *-tion*, your final list should include at least a couple of words that are considered *morphologically challenging*—those words that can change forms and meaning through adding or taking away affixes. Alternatively, you may notice that only two words have multiple meanings, and therefore you decide they automatically make the cut because you have recently been focusing on strengthening your students' understanding that the same word can mean something different depending on the way it's used. Then again, you may look down your list and find that two words have very similar meanings—the study of two very similar words within the same instructional cycle can be a potential "liability" for word learning—so you know you need to cut one and save it for a later instructional cycle (Nagy and Hiebert 2011). Whatever the case, select those terms that, when taught as a group, will best support your ELs' literacy development.

FINALIZE YOUR LIST

Teacher: Ms. Bruno

Grade Level: 4

Big Idea: Ethical Treatment of Animals

Touchstone Text: *Zoos Then and Now*

	USEFULNESS					COMPLEXITY		
Selected Target Words*	For This Text	For This Big Idea	For Big Ideas to Come	Across Content Areas	In a Particular Content Area	Conceptually Abstract	Polysemous	Morphologically Challenging
exhibit This word is crucial to text comprehension and has related morphological variants (e.g., *exhibition*). In addition, this word has morphological derivations that change the word's part of speech (e.g., *exhibit* as a noun or a verb, and the derivation *exhibition* as a noun) and appears multiple times in the touchstone text.	✓			✓		✓	✓	✓
environment This word can be used in multiple ways (the *environment* as the sum of ecological influences, such as climate, soil, and other life forms versus an *environment* as one's surroundings or conditions), has morphological derivations (e.g., *environmental*), and also appears more than once in the touchstone text.	✓	✓	✓	✓	✓	✓	✓	✓

continues

Figure 6.5 Step 3 in Action

	USEFULNESS					COMPLEXITY		
Selected Target Words	For This Text	For This Big Idea	For Big Ideas to Come	Across Content Areas	In a Particular Content Area	Conceptually Abstract	Polysemous	Morphologically Challenging
impact This word is central to understanding the selection, appears twice in the touchstone text, and has the potential to appear in multiple content areas (e.g., science: the impact of the moon on tides).	✓	✓	✓	✓	✓	✓	✓	
promotes While this word appears only once in the text, it is common across content areas and can be used multiple ways (e.g., *promote* as in supporting the growth or development of something or someone or *promote* as in moving up in position or rank). The morphological variants (e.g., *promotion*) also make the word a strong candidate for this instruction.	✓	✓	✓	✓		✓	✓	✓

Figure 6.5 Step 3 in Action *(continued)*

Selected Target Words	USEFULNESS					COMPLEXITY		
	For This Text	For This Big Idea	For Big Ideas to Come	Across Content Areas	In a Particular Content Area	Conceptually Abstract	Polysemous	Morphologically Challenging
pursuit This word appears twice in the text and is important for comprehending the conclusion. Additionally, idiomatic expressions (e.g., *in hot pursuit*) extend the word's usage beyond its applicability in this particular context.	✓			✓			✓	
investigation While this word appears only once in the touchstone text, it offers potential for multiple uses across the content areas (e.g., *investigation* as in conducting a systematic scientific experiment or as in conducting a criminal inquiry). The morphological variants (e.g., *investigate, investigator*) also make the word a strong candidate for instruction.			✓	✓				✓

*Target word selections and descriptions drawn from the What Works Clearinghouse guide, *Teaching Academic Content and Literacy to English Learners in Elementary and Middle Grades* (Baker et al. 2014).

Figure 6.5 Step 3 in Action *(continued)*

What's Ms. Parkin's final list?

Narrowing things down and making final decisions are neither Ms. Parkin's favorite tasks nor always her strong suit, but a process does help somewhat. In this case, finalizing her list was especially difficult because the majority of the words she recorded were useful, complex, or both. Ultimately, here's how she narrowed things down: Easily enough, she first eliminated those words that didn't meet some basic criteria, including useful across content areas; conceptually abstract; central to the big idea.

Although she didn't feel that *shadow* and *reflect* were particularly salient to the cycle's big idea, she wants to focus instruction on multiple meanings, and these two polysemous words would be perfect for that goal. In that sense, they were related *enough* to the big idea. She decided not to cross those two off just yet. Then, she continued with the words that were left:

- She marked off words related to terms and concepts in previous and upcoming instructional cycles (e.g., *disguise*).
- She marked off those with a morphological transformation in common. Of the words that were left on her list, several could be combined with the suffix *-able*: *disguise*, *survive*, *recognize*, *adaptation*, and *attract*. Because the complexity of this particular suffix matches nicely with her third-grade learning goals, she was set.

Going through this multistep process resulted in this final list of target words:

- *pattern*
- *shadow*
- *surface*
- *reflect*
- *disguise*
- *survive/survivor*
- *recognize*
- *attract/attractive*
- *environment*
- *adapt/adaptation*

Deep Word Study: One More Piece

Developing ELs' academic vocabulary knowledge by focusing each knowledge-building cycle on a (well-selected!) set of target words that correspond with the cycle's big idea and touchstone text is foundational to strong literacy instruction in linguistically diverse classrooms. But this deep word study is not complete without one more piece: explicit attention to the relationships among words and how to leverage these relationships in the service of independent word learning. In fact, for ELs, this element of knowledge-building instruction is so important that we devote a full chapter to it; Chapter 7 focuses on supporting ELs to be expert word learners. In the chapter, we discuss how to arm ELs with the tools and skills they need to unlock the meaning of unfamiliar words so that their word knowledge continually expands and deepens, throughout the day and across the many places (e.g., home, school, community) where word learning can occur.

PROTOCOLS FOR PLANNING AND REFLECTION

Word Selection Matrix

Big Idea: ____________________

Touchstone Text: ____________________

Potential Target Words	USEFULNESS					COMPLEXITY		
	For This Text	For This Big Idea	For Big Ideas to Come	Across Content Areas	In a Particular Content Area	Conceptually Abstract	Polysemous	Morphologically Challenging

7

Unlock Language by Developing Word-Learning Strategies

As English learners (ELs) progress through the grades, the curriculum will continue to include more and more words that are unfamiliar to them, many of which will represent abstract concepts. For all students, not just ELs, it's just not possible to provide them with direct instruction in *all* of the words they need to be deeply familiar with. In other words, we can't teach them the roughly three thousand new words they need to learn *each year* to keep pace with the school curriculum (Nagy, Anderson, and Herman 1987). There just isn't time and it wouldn't be practical—it would also be a challenge to keep this engaging, for that matter!

But we can support ELs to be excellent word learners. We can arm them with the tools and skills to unlock the meaning of unfamiliar words and heighten their awareness of the printed and spoken words around them so that their word knowledge—and world knowledge—continually deepens. ELs need tools in their kit that reflect a command of how words work and strategies to figure out the meaning of unfamiliar words, especially while reading independently. Therefore, instruction that cultivates knowledge—and therefore supports advanced literacy development—necessarily includes a focus on developing word-learning strategies. When we unlock language by developing ELs' word-learning strategies, we are tightening the link between classroom instruction and ELs' literacy strengths and needs, advancing their vocabulary, reading, and writing development. In the linguistically diverse knowledge-building classroom, there are at least four key *word-learning strategies*:

- breaking words into meaningful parts
- using clues present in surrounding text
- consciously attending to words
- making connections to native language.

In taking this approach to literacy instruction, a focus on word learning is embedded throughout the instructional cycle, but we also carve out the time to bring word-learning strategy instruction to the forefront of our teaching. In this way, from cycle to cycle, we are unlocking language for ELs and their classmates, equipping them with the knowledge of how words and language work—knowledge that we cannot assume is intuitive or latent.

Break words into meaningful parts

A capacity to reflect on and manipulate the meaningful parts within words—e.g.,roots, suffixes, and prefixes—allows students to dissect complex words into more familiar parts and in turn decipher their (likely) meanings. Often referred to as *morphological awareness*, this skill is a key tool to understand the relationship between words, e.g., *popular* and *popularity*; *constant* and *inconstancy*; *detective* and *detect*.

Use clues present in surrounding text

Context clues can sometimes help students derive personal, yet workable definitions of unfamiliar words using any surrounding text that is familiar and understood.

Consciously attend to words

When we foster ELs' curiosity in the words they hear and see—encouraging them to attend to language, play with words, and share interesting word encounters—they are primed to deepen and broaden their word knowledge, throughout the day and across the many places (e.g., home, school, community) that learning can happen.

Make connections to native language

Learning to identify similarities between English words and words in their primary language can help ELs to infer unknown word meanings on their own. These cross-language links are most often in the form of *cognates*: Words that share a common origin in two or more languages. For example, in Spanish, *electricidad* means electricity and *organismo* means organism.

Baker et al. 2014

Figure 7.1 What word-learning strategies can we foster?

Our Focus in This Knowledge-Building Approach: Morphology (with a Little Context)

For those of you who have worked on building up students' word-learning strategies, you might be thinking about strategies like context clues and inferencing skills. These can be viable and effective, but often only for our strongest readers. Here in this book about knowledge-building literacy instruction for ELs, based on a robust body of research, we focus the majority of our attention on one word-learning strategy in particular: building up students' morphological awareness skills. We focus a little on context clues but only as part of a larger approach that privileges morphology.

Why morphology? Well, recent research conducted with ELs confirms what we've learned from research conducted with monolingual English-speaking

MORPHOLOGY: A PRIMER

In language and reading, morphology refers to the study of the structure of words, particularly the smallest units of meaning in words: morphemes. Morphemes are generally one of three types:

- roots that can stand alone as words, such as *popular* in *popularity*, *constant* in *inconstancy*, and *detect* in *detective*
- roots that cannot stand alone as words, like Latin and Greek roots such as *audi*, *ology*, and *tele*
- prefixes and suffixes that cannot stand alone as words, such as *–ity*, *in-*, *and -ive.*

The latter category of morphemes, prefixes and suffixes, can be further broken down into two categories:

- inflectional suffixes such as *-ed* and *-s* that change the tense or number of a word without changing its part of speech
- derivational prefixes and suffixes such as *un-*, *-ity*, and *-tion* that change a word's part of speech or shade of meaning.

When our instruction targets ELs' *morphological awareness*, then we are developing their ability to reflect on and manipulate the meaningful parts within words, including roots, suffixes, and prefixes.

students: There is a reciprocal relationship between morphology skills and meaning-based literacy competencies (Carlisle 2000; Deacon and Kirby 2004; Goodwin et al. 2013; Kieffer, Biancarosa, and Mancilla-Martinez 2013; Nagy, Berninger, and Abbott 2006).

- **Vocabulary.** ELs with larger vocabularies tend to have greater understanding of morphology, and the relationship between vocabulary and morphology appears to be reciprocal (Kieffer and Lesaux 2007). Understanding how words work appears to help students broaden their vocabularies, and vocabulary growth may improve students' understanding of morphology. And both domains of knowledge relate strongly to reading comprehension.
- **Reading.** Like vocabulary, reading comprehension and morphological awareness appear to have a reciprocal relationship. The strength of this relationship grows as students move up through the grades (Kieffer and Lesaux 2007; Kirby et al. 2012). In fact, by fifth grade, a student's knowledge of morphology can predict his reading comprehension level (Goodwin et al. 2013; Kieffer and Lesaux 2008). It therefore stands to reason that if, from the earliest grades, we embark on supporting the developmental sequence of language learning and focus on the long-term process of developing this language skill, ELs will become more proficient readers.
- **Writing.** There is also some evidence that when ELs have a better grasp of how words work, they also have a more precise understanding of how to use words in their different forms in different sentences and move more flexibly between these forms. For example, imagine a student is writing to describe how animals survive in their environments. She might initially write, "animal adaptations to where they live." When rereading her work, she might notice that this sentence just isn't quite right. She could then apply her morphological awareness skills to break apart the word *adaptations*, attempting a syntactically accurate use of this term.

How Do I Develop English Learners' Word-Learning Strategies?

Teach Cognitive Steps for Supporting Word-Learning Strategies

Sharpening ELs' capacities to unlock the meaning of unfamiliar words means promoting a way of thinking about language. When reading, this means monitoring for meaning and having a set of cognitive steps to undertake when faced

DEVELOPING WORD-LEARNING STRATEGIES: A STRENGTHS-BASED INSTRUCTIONAL APPROACH

Beyond its practical importance, building up ELs' word-learning strategies also fits into a strengths-based perspective on teaching—a perspective that fuels strong teaching and learning, but that historically has not always been adopted when teaching ELs (e.g., Gándara et al. 2003). That is, equipping ELs with the knowledge and strategies it takes to unlock language is well matched with key strengths that current research tells us about this population:

Learning rates	ELs' rates of growth in language development surpass the rates of their peers (Kieffer 2008, 2010; Mancilla-Martinez and Lesaux 2011). That is, while they may be learning more words than their peers throughout the schooling years, the problem is that many of their monolingual English-speaking classmates started out with more words. So, although many ELs might not "catch up" to their monolingual English-speaking peers over time, we know that, for the vast majority this is not an "ability to learn" problem.
Active-learner stance	Emerging research and teachers' experiences tell us that many ELs are very actively engaged in the meaning-making process when reading and listening: making inferences, connecting what they read to what they know, and searching for answers (García 1991; Harris and Lesaux 2014). We can tap this active-learner stance by equipping students with strategies that are squarely focused on language learning.
Knowledge of languages (plural!)	Many ELs are well beyond the beginning stages of English proficiency and are navigating two languages. Although the degree to which ELs are proficient in their first language certainly varies, their first-language skills are an asset. When we equip ELs with word-learning skills that invoke their native language proficiency, they'll be tuned in to the fact that a subset of the "new" words they encounter in print are actually understandable when they find cognate connections that unlock the meaning.

with an unfamiliar word or phrase. These cognitive steps involve deploying the word-learning tools described previously (e.g., breaking words into meaningful parts and using clues present in surround text), in a strategic manner, to support comprehension in real time.

So what are specific cognitive steps for unlocking language? In collaboration with Michael Kieffer, Nonie has developed and written about four cognitive steps that ELs can practice and use, featured in Figure 7.2 (Kieffer and Lesaux 2007, 2010). Nonie and Michael view these steps as a "series of stages in thinking." Teachers should teach these four thinking stages explicitly, explain to ELs how they are useful in their own word learning, model them several times with meaningful examples, and provide students with time and guidance to practice them (Kieffer and Lesaux 2007, 2010).

What does this look like in Ms. Parkin's classroom?

The third graders we met in earlier chapters, Javier, Camilla, Mateo and their classmates, are in a learning environment that is tuned into the different ways we unlock language for meaning. For example, next to the academic word wall is a poster that lays out different cognitive steps for word learning—an ever-present reminder that students have the tools it takes to decipher the meanings of

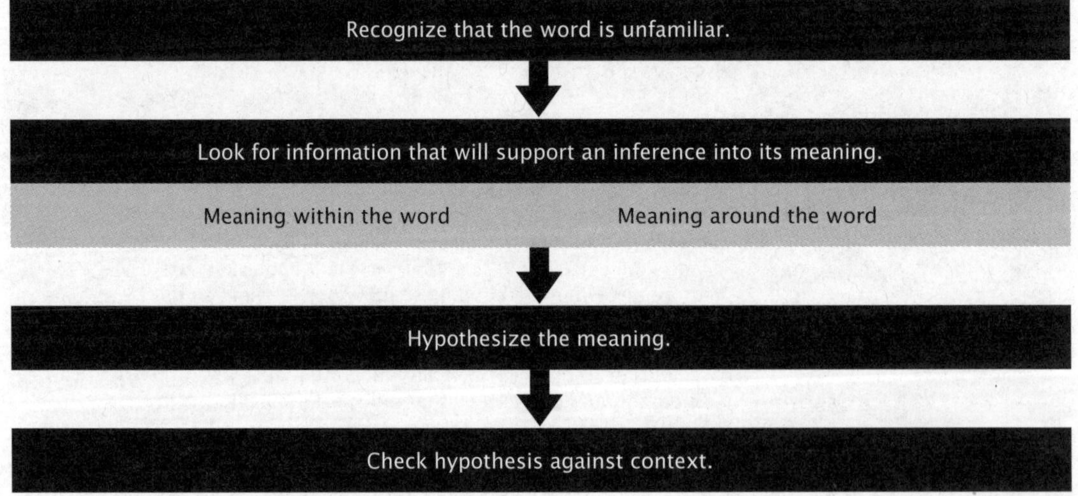

Figure 7.2 Cognitive Steps for Unlocking Language

unfamiliar words. These steps have been part of their collective work since early in the year, when Ms. Parkin and her students were learning the routines associated with cycle's learning tasks (see Chapter 4). She recalls back to when, as an entry point, she modeled the steps using a familiar read-aloud, putting the steps into action. Then, after trying them out together and engaging in a carousel brainstorming activity that would become part and parcel of their knowledge-building cycle (see Chapter 4), in small groups, they circulated to "clue hunt stations." Here, sentences containing likely unfamiliar words were posted. At each station, students had the chance to practice the steps in a challenging, yet doable, context. Here is an example:

- The newspaper reporter is going to write about the election because it is an important, *newsworthy* story.
- When I looked at the *sandstone*, I could see the pieces of sand stuck together inside of the rock.
- A green puffer fish is almost all green with black spots. However, its *underbelly*, or stomach, is white.
- When the singer walked on the stage, the *footlights* on the floor shined so we could see her sing.
- Let's go to the new *waterside* restaurant. You know, the one at the edge of the lake.

Notice how the word parts (in this case, two roots joined to form compound words) and context clues are relatively easy to find to keep this straightforward and positive in this initial phase? Students brought their own clipboard with recording sheets to each station, to note the word part and context clues that provided useful information for hypothesizing the meaning of the unfamiliar word (in italics). They hypothesize on their own, and then as a group. The recording sheet looked something like this:

Unlocking Word Meanings: Student Recording Sheet

Unknown Word	Word Parts	Context Clues	Now, What Do You Think the Word Means?
newsworthy	*news* *worthy*	Newspaper Important story	A story that's important enough to be in the news

After each group visited all of the stations, the class came back together to discuss the process. Of course, this interactive activity was only the beginning. While this "clue hunt" familiarized Ms. Parkin's students with the cognitive steps for unlocking language (and the classroom procedures for this interactive learning task), in the months that followed, Ms. Parkin also modeled the steps in other ways, always referring to the visual reminder on the wall and encouraging her students during guided reading groups to put the steps into action. She also carved out the time in each instructional cycle to build her students' morphological knowledge—a more sophisticated, nuanced approach to word learning. The next section describes what that means and what that looks like.

SPOTLIGHT ON FINDING MEANING AROUND THE WORD (AKA CONTEXT CLUES)

One of the cognitive steps for unlocking language revolves around finding meaning around the word: using clues present in surrounding text to support hypothesis making about a word's meaning. These clues, as standalone sources of information, can support accurate hypothesis making for some readers, but often only for our strongest readers. In the approach we are describing here, context clues are taught as part of a larger approach to word-learning strategy instruction to accommodate diversity among our readers, including ELs and their peers struggling with reading comprehension—one that privileges morphology.

That said, for research-based, practical advice on supporting students to successfully use context clues, we turn to a framework by James Baumann and colleagues, focused on thinking about and teaching this sometimes elusive idea of context clues (e.g., Baumann et al. 2003). Within this framework, there are five types of context clues (see chart; Baumann et al. 2003, 465). In the far right column, we listed some examples that you might share with your students when describing what context clues are all about. The bolded words are the potentially unfamiliar word, and the underlined phrases are the clues. For more guidance on teaching context clues, see other work by Baumann and colleagues, including their *Reading Teacher* article, "'Bumping into Spicy, Tasty Words That Catch Your Tongue': A Formative Experiment on Vocabulary Instruction" (Baumann, Ware, and Edwards 2007).

Build Knowledge of Meaningful Word Parts and Word Relationships

Effectively using cognitive steps for unlocking word meanings requires a certain amount of knowledge about words themselves. For that reason, our teaching must make visible the ways in which information within a word can illuminate meaning. These within-word clues take two forms:

- **Parts of the word that carry meaning or signal relationships to other words in English.** The most common within-word clues are *morphemes*: the smallest units of meaning in words, such as roots, suffixes, and prefixes. An understanding of morphology can be a powerful tool for students

Context Clue Type	When the Author . . .	Example
Definition	. . . gives you a definition for a word right in the sentence	**Mammoths**, hairy elephants, lived during the Ice Age.
Synonym	. . . uses another word that means about the same thing as the word you are trying to understand	When my partner and I couldn't find our science project, I was **frantic**. My partner was very worried as well.
Antonym	. . . uses another word that means the opposite or nearly the opposite of the word you are trying to understand	Sometimes word problems in math class are very **intricate**. I wish they were simple instead.
Example	. . . gives you several words or ideas that are examples of the word you are trying to understand	The fifth grade was full of **precocious** children. One child had learned geometry at age six, and another could read at age two.
General	. . . gives you some general clues to the meaning of a word, often spread over several sentences	**Manipulation** of members of the student council is not allowed. Everyone must let them decide what to do with the money raised.

faced with the daunting task of acquiring academic vocabulary. A large number of the unfamiliar words that students encounter in print could be deciphered if students knew the more common root word and could break the complex word down into meaningful, familiar parts.

- **Parts of the word that are related to words in an EL's native language.** These cross-language links are most often in the form of *cognates*: words in two or more languages that share a common origin. This element of linguistic knowledge is most useful for those students whose primary languages comprise a considerable number of words with similar spellings and meaning in English, such as Spanish, Portuguese, and other Romance languages.

TEACHING MEANINGFUL WORD PARTS: IT'S NOT JUST AN ADOLESCENT THING

Our youngest children are always playing with words—it's part of development! They generally understand or are learning about more simple suffixes (such as *-s* on plurals or *-ed* on past-tense verbs) and compound words, and so working explicitly and systematically on their word-learning strategies turns out to be developmentally appropriate. For this reason, playing with language by breaking words apart and making new ones can be incredibly fruitful in classrooms with younger children. When designed with ELs' developmental and language-learning stages in mind, instruction focused on developing word-learning strategies can, and should, be used with our youngest learners (Bowers, Kirby, and Deacon 2010) and our adolescents. We know that there has been a bit of buzz around teaching adolescents about word parts (morphology), but for this teaching to be really effective, it should start much sooner. Figure 7.3 presents the most common prefixes and suffixes, in order of frequency (adapted from Blevins 2001; Kieffer and Lesaux 2007). You can match the frequency levels of the word parts you teach to the language levels of your students, beginning with the most common word parts.

PREFIXES		
High Frequency	**Medium Frequency**	**Low Frequency**
un- (not, opposite of)	*over-* (too much)	*trans-* (across)
re- (again)	*mis-* (wrongly)	*super-* (above)
in-, im-, ir-, il- (not)	*sub-* (under)	*semi-* (half)
dis- (not, opposite of)	*pre-* (before)	*anti-* (against)
en-, em- (cause to)	*inter-* (between, among)	*mid-* (middle)
non- (not)		
under- (too little)		
in-, im- (in or into)		
SUFFIXES		
High Frequency	**Medium Frequency**	**Low Frequency**
-s (plurals)	*-ly* (characteristic of)	*-al, -ial* (having characteristics of)
-ed (past tense)	*-er, -or* (person)	*-y* (characterized by)
-ing (present tense)	*-ion, -tion* (act, process)	*-ness* (state of, condition of)
	-ible, -able (can be done)	*-ity, -ty* (state of)
		-ment (action or process)
		-ic (having characteristics of)
		-ous, -eous, -ious (possessing the qualities of)
		-en (made of)
		-ive, -ative, -itive (adjective form of a noun)
		-ful (full of)
		-less (without)

Blevins 2001; Kieffer and Lesaux 2007

Figure 7.3 Most Common Prefixes and Suffixes in Order of Frequency

What does this look like in Ms. Parkin's classroom?

Let's once again visit Ms. Parkin's classroom. Recall that in Chapter 6, she decided on the target words for her knowledge-building cycle, focused on how animals survive in their environments. These included: *pattern, shadow, surface, reflect, disguise, survive/survivor, recognize, attract/attractive, environment,* and *adapt/*

adaptation. In finalizing her set of target words, she was aware that a number of the words could be combined with the suffix *-able*; this relationship to the cycle was key because she wanted to be sure that students could practice breaking down and forming words in authentic contexts. But that's not all—what makes *-able* a strong candidate is that it is a relatively high-frequency suffix (compared to, say, *-ive*, which was also a candidate) and therefore a good match for her students' stage in the developmental sequence of language learning.

So, what does Ms. Parkin do to support her students' knowledge of word parts that carry meaning? First, she introduces the word part using common examples (e.g., *likeable, enjoyable*), and then moves to new forms of their academic target words (e.g., *recognizable, survivable*). Next, she turns to a core, evidence-based learning task in her classroom: recording word forms on a classroom word form chart (Harmon et al. 2009; Kieffer and Lesaux 2010). As shown in Figure 7.4, a word form chart is a simple chart on which students and their teacher record the new morphological forms of words they learn according to their part of speech and thus their function in sentences. It's both interactive and cumulative; as new word parts are introduced and as students encounter or create new words with previously taught prefixes or suffixes, Ms. Parkin and her students record them. Note that in this case, Ms. Parkin and her students also recorded the multiple forms that target words appeared in the touchstone text (e.g., *attract* and *attractive*; *survive* and *survivor*).

Next, Ms. Parkin provides opportunities for supported practice. In a previous unit, when Ms. Parkin taught the suffix *-er*, she initially offered students the opportunity to practice identifying and working with this suffix using a word sort activity. Students sorted words ending in *-er* according to their meaning: words whereby the

Verbs (actions)	**Nouns** (person, place, thing, or idea)	**Adjectives** (words to describe nouns)	**Adverbs** (words to describe actions)
adapt	adaptation	adaptable	
attract		attractive attractable	
disguise		disguisable	
recognize		recognizable	
survive	survivor	survivable	

Figure 7.4 Ms. Parkin's Word Form Chart

added suffix changes a verb such that it now refers to a person or thing; words in which the suffix is used to compare (e.g., *bigger*); and those words in which the *-er* is part of the root (e.g., the words *mother*, *bother*, and *deer*). This time around, Ms. Parkin's students engaged in a word hunt using a short, thematically related text that they had read the day prior. In pairs, students searched for words with *-able* and used the cognitive steps previously described to infer their meanings.

The following week, Ms. Parkin introduced a new literacy center: writing captions containing target words with *-able*, describing photographs and illustrations related to the cycle's theme: animals they had encountered in the touchstone text and the adaptations they exhibit.

ANOTHER APPROACH: COLLABORATIVE STRATEGIC READING

Another (related) way to think about developing ELs' cognitive strategies for unlocking meaning is embedded in a technique for improving comprehension called "collaborative strategic reading" (Klingner et al. 2012). This instructional approach, which enjoys considerable research support, involves guiding and supporting students to use four comprehension strategies simultaneously (e.g., Klingner, Vaughn, and Schumm 1998; Klingner et al. 2004). One of these strategies is called "click and clunk." When, applying this strategy during reading, students are encouraged to tune into what makes sense, "clicks," and what doesn't seem to make sense, "clunks." Much like the steps developed by Michael and Nonie, the cognitive steps involved in the click and clunk strategy integrate the word-learning strategies highlighted at the opening of this chapter: breaking words into parts, using clues present in surrounding text, and making connections to your native language. What are the cognitive steps of "click and clunk"?

- Identify clunks.
- Use fix-up strategies to figure out the meaning of the clunks.
  - Reread the sentence with the clunk, and look for key ideas to help you figure out the word. Think about what makes sense.
  - Reread the sentences before and after the clunk, looking for clues.
  - Look for a root word, prefix, or suffix in the word that might help.
  - Look for a cognate that makes sense.

Things to Keep in Mind

We've certainly stressed the importance of developing ELs' word-learning strategies, but like all approaches, this strategy instruction also has its pitfalls. So, let's keep two issues in mind:

1. Word-learning strategies are intended to be taught and practiced through interactive learning opportunities that are related to the big ideas being studied. These strategies are only useful as tools in an instructional cycle focused on content learning. If we stray too far from our primary goal of building up students' knowledge by conducting strategy instruction in isolation, rather than integrating it into a knowledge-building cycle, our teaching and learning will fall far short.
2. Another potential pitfall of this approach is that students fall into the habit of overapplying word-learning strategies, especially without checking inferred meanings against the context (Kieffer and Lesaux 2010). For instance, students who have been taught that the suffix *-er* makes a word "refer to a person who does a particular action or has a particular job" might be confused by *dreamier* if they do not learn that this suffix can also mean "more than" and develop the skills to decide which meaning is appropriate. We need to teach this example and the larger lesson, lest they get frustrated or simply go down the wrong road trying to decipher *embroider*, *meter*, or *boulder*. There are few hard-and-fast rules, particularly in English, but the more tools we give our students—especially our ELs—through authentic practice, the better their chances of developing advanced literacy skills. We raise our students' awareness of these pitfalls and support them to be able to use strategies wisely.

Unlocking Language: From Comprehension to Communication

Supporting ELs to develop the word-learning strategies described in this chapter puts them on a path to becoming expert word learners. But that's not all. As we mentioned earlier, when ELs have a better grasp of how words work, they also have a more precise understanding of how to use words in their different forms in different sentences and move more flexibly between these forms. In the next chapter, we talk much more about what it means to support ELs to communicate their thinking around the cycle's big idea using oral and written academic language.

PROTOCOLS FOR PLANNING AND REFLECTION

Selecting Word Parts for Instruction

Potential target-word parts: ___________________________

How this word part affects meaning and usage: ___________________________

Is this word part a good fit for this cycle and my students?	Notes to Self
☐ Relevant to target words in this cycle ☐ Relevant to target words in previous cycles ☐ Appropriate level of complexity for my students Use the chart on page 117 as a guide to gauge this word part's frequency in the English language. ☐ High ☐ Medium ☐ Low	

Designing Morphology Instruction

Building Students' Knowledge of Word Parts	**Instructional Planning**
Explicit Instruction	
☐ Introduce target-word part using common example(s)	Common examples:
☐ Connect to target words	Target word connections:
☐ Use Word Form Chart as a tool to discuss and record how word parts change part of speech	
☐ Connect to native language (when applicable)	Native language connections:
Supported Student Practice	
☐ Provide opportunities for students to identify, decipher, and transform words using new word parts	Learning tasks that provide supported practice:
☐ Provide practice in talking and writing with new word forms	
☐ Provide opportunities for students to apply their new word-part knowledge by designing activities/tasks with unfamiliar words (see the Cognitive Steps for Unlocking Language on page 112.)	

Extend Learning with Language Production Projects

As we close this book, we now turn to a strategy that's probably the most neglected, but absolutely key to creating a knowledge-building classroom: extending learning with *language production projects*. These projects offer English learners (ELs) and their classmates the opportunity to consolidate and extend their understanding of the content studied over the course of the instructional cycle. They can and should often take the form of capstone projects—those that are the culminating or crowning experiences and achievements for the unit of study. But they don't have to. With the right setup and support, we can engage students in projects on any given day and at any point in our instructional calendar. Next, we describe what we mean by *language production projects*, the ways in which they extend student learning, and how to design them.

What Do We Mean by *Language Production Projects*?

A *language production project* is a content-based, purpose-driven opportunity to craft (i.e., plan, generate, and revise) an oral or written product. Depending on the cycle's big idea and students' developmental stage, a language production project could take many forms: a debate, letter-writing campaign, public service announcement, mock trial, presentation, or even some kind of performance (e.g., giving a speech). Whether the project primarily involves oral or written language, a defining feature is that students work on these projects over an extended period of time.

In the knowledge-building classroom, producing language is part and parcel of the school day. These opportunities for ELs and their peers to engage in academic discourse exist across a continuum from brief to extensive, occurring more or less frequently depending upon the scope and purpose of the learning task. All of these opportunities—from quick sharing to collaborative literacy centers to large thematic projects—matter for developing advanced literacy skills, and all are crucial components of knowledge-building literacy instruction. But projects organized around language production are distinct from other language production activities and tasks. These projects are the focus of this chapter.

What does this look like in Ms. Parkin's classroom?

The most exciting task for Ms. Parkin was designing the language production project that would cap the cycle on how animals survive in their environments. In all her years, it's this project-based work—about something her students have a good grasp on and really care about—that most brings her classroom of learners to life. The energy is contagious, and it's such a fulfilling experience to see the prep in action.

But coming up with the specifics of each project always feels a little daunting at first: She wants her students to get a lot out of this experience, and much like deciding on a touchstone text, without her goals clearly outlined, she can sometimes get lost in the possibilities. Based on her goals for her students, she needs to design a project that will provide them with the support and opportunities to research a topic, generate a written text that communicates what they found and why it matters, including using the target words (e.g., *disguise, pattern, adapt*, etc.), and then reflect on and revise that text. She also wants to provide her students with the chance to present what they created—reporting on their topic to an interested audience and fielding questions from the audience. Of course, this research project will connect to the cycle's big idea, but she has to decide how the project will extend students' content knowledge. She's thinking about the issue of how changes in habitats, whether induced by the climate and/or humans, affect the organisms that live there, thereby affecting the organisms' survival.

How Do Language Production Projects Extend Learning?

Unlike the all-too-familiar speaking and writing assignments many of us remember from our own schooling experiences (e.g., responding to prompts about our summer vacations and assignments about our favorite U.S. state—or in Nonie's case, Canadian province!), language production projects aren't strictly meant to fill time, and they do much more than ask students to complete a task that is isolated from the rest of their classroom learning experiences. When used in concert with the other strategies described throughout this book, and therefore are an integral part of a knowledge-building approach to literacy instruction, language production projects *extend* learning—and in more ways than one. They promote students':

- **written language skills.** It goes without saying that providing our students with opportunities to write, and supporting them in the writing process, has an impact on written language skills. But when we support writing in the context of a content-based project—one that involves students in purposeful inquiry, analysis, and explanation—we take that development a step further (Graham, Gillespie, and McKeown 2013). Not to mention, when students simultaneously practice their *oral* language skills (through peer collaboration), their written language skills improve even more (Graham, Gillespie, and McKeown 2013).
- **oral language skills.** Though the research base is still disappointingly thin, the evidence we do have—coupled with professional wisdom—points to the importance of "speaking to learn" in classrooms. We simply cannot expect ELs to increase their English language proficiency if we do not provide supportive opportunities to craft and present arguments for debate, speeches for performance, and other spoken explanations of their learning (Baker et al. 2014).
- **reading comprehension skills.** Producing language in the context of a content-based and purpose-driven project supports not only written and oral language development but also reading comprehension. Of note, a recent meta-analysis highlights the impact of writing instruction, and writing in connection with content learning in particular, on students' text comprehension (Graham and Hebert 2011).
- **content area knowledge.** These projects provide a prime, even essential, context for deepening our learners' content area knowledge. When students engage in a scaffolded, collaborative, multiday process of planning

and generating a written or spoken product, their understanding of the big idea under study improves (Bangert-Drowns, Hurley, and Wilkinson 2004; Graham, Gillespie, and McKeown 2013; Halvorsen et al. 2012; Lawrence and Snow 2011; Taylor and Duke 2013).

- **academic motivation.** Language production projects integrate many of the instructional strategies known to increase students' academic motivation: They can provide personal relevance, choice, and meaningful collaboration (Guthrie 2011). When implemented as a capstone to a knowledge-building cycle revolving around a conceptually complex big idea, they also provide the (well-earned!) chance to step into the role of expert. Generating a written or spoken product that extends from a knowledge-building instructional cycle provides ELs with an opportunity to witness their own academic progress, and this experience of progress provides a valuable and motivating sense of efficacy and confidence (Lesaux, Harris, and Sloane 2012). For our ELs and their classroom peers who otherwise view themselves as not so good at this thing called *school*, the confidence that comes with fruitful efforts and a product to be proud of is invaluable.

How Do I Design Language Production Projects That Extend Learning?

Now that we've discussed some of their key benefits, let's focus on what is meant, exactly, by a language production project, because just any project won't necessarily extend ELs' academic content knowledge and meaning-based literacy skills. Instead, there are several key features that make these projects stand out among the rest. Two primary lines of scholarship bring these features to the surface: practice-based scholarship focused on motivation and instructional design (e.g., Duke et al. 2012; Guthrie 2011; Taylor and Duke 2013) and research focused specifically on academic language instruction with ELs (Baker et al. 2014). The first line of thinking tells us to be sure to organize the project around a compelling purpose. The second line of research tells us we need to anchor language production projects in the instructional cycle's big idea and to encourage and support use of target vocabulary words.

Organize the Project Around a Compelling Purpose

Scholars in the fields of motivation and content area literacy remind us of the importance of designing language production projects that are driven by compelling purposes for communicating with others (Duke et al. 2006; Guthrie 2011). Whatever the purpose, ELs then use the project as a means to achieve it. As Ms. Parkin's students work toward completing their project, her ELs and their peers will be driven by intention—one that is related to the cycle's big idea. A purpose can take many forms; some possibilities for purpose and some of Ms. Parkin's thinking during her capstone planning include:

- conveying information to an audience students really want to connect with (e.g., the local mayor who is organizing a housing development that will change amphibian habitats)
- learning more about an aspect of the big idea that students really care about (e.g., how climate changes may be influencing birds' migration patterns and survival)
- solving a problem that concerns students (e.g., animal welfare and survival in the local ecosystem)
- making sense of scientific phenomena, social issues, and identities (e.g., climate change, urban development, protecting threatened and endangered species).

Anchor Language Production Projects in the Instructional Cycle's Big Idea

As you might recall from Chapter 4, a key strategy for promoting ELs' advanced literacy skills is to provide instructional consistency by organizing lessons within a knowledge-building cycle and to be sure there is a multifaceted, content-based, and engaging topic—a big idea—at the heart of each cycle (Figures 8.1 and 8.2). By studying one big idea throughout the cycle, ELs and their peers engage in the process of deep learning.

It follows, then, that as the knowledge-building cycle progresses and students are reading, talking, and thinking critically about a particular big idea, they are gaining knowledge and building up the understanding it takes to express that knowledge and make it their own. When ELs have built up a firm and nuanced foundation about a topic, then the project becomes a platform for advancing learning. After all, no matter how meaningful or interesting the assignment, generating an oral or written product will not optimally extend learning if this process does not follow the deep study of the topic at hand.

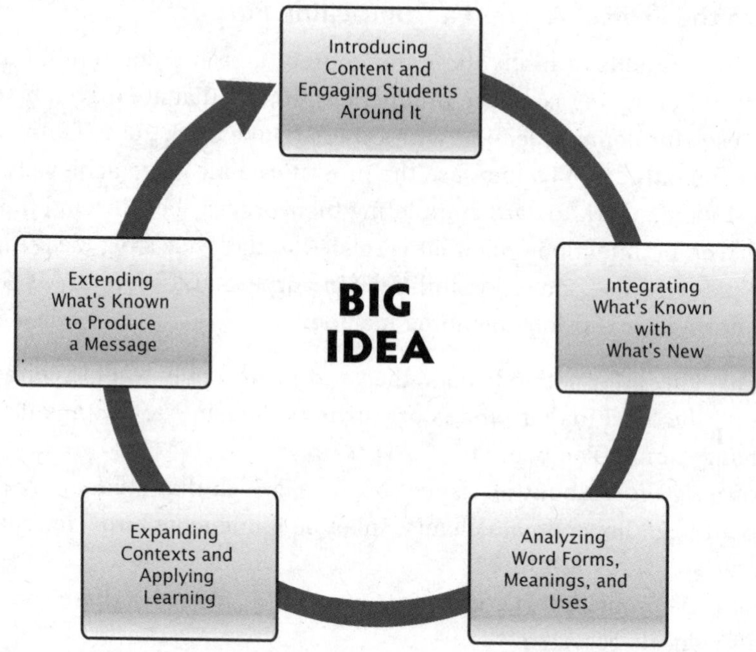

Figure 8.1 Chapter 4 Recap: Developmental Sequence for Building Up Knowledge

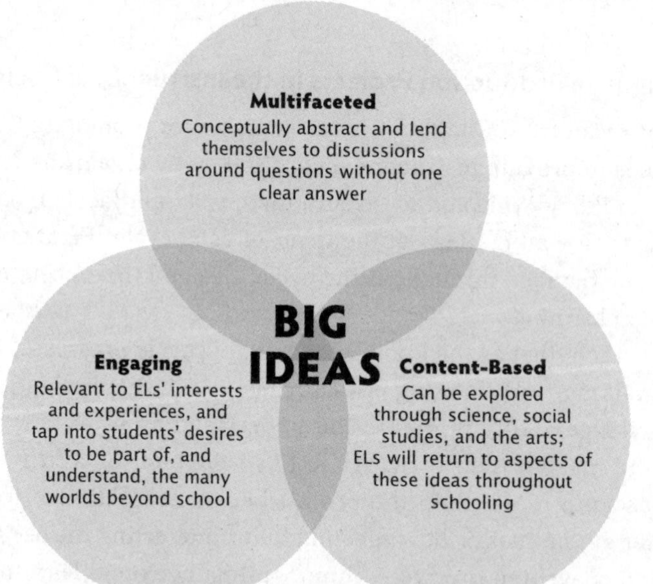

Figure 8.2 Chapter 5 Recap: What Makes Big Ideas *Big*?

Figure 8.3 features the language production project that Ms. Parkin ultimately decides to use to reinforce and extend her students' understanding of animal survival and adaptation, while building language skills. For this project, she is supporting students to learn about and generate solutions to a local issue: How can communities support animals' survival in modern, urban environments?

Topic	▪ How can we better coexist with wildlife?
What compelling issue will students focus on?	▪ How can we be "good neighbors" to animals, supporting their survival in and around our community?
What research will they need to undertake?	▪ Document dangers that animals face every day (e.g., snowy owls mistake the low and flat land around the nearby airport for the Arctic tundra; migrating birds that collide with illuminated windows of high-rise buildings; and salamanders and frogs that migrate to vernal pools, i.e., seasonal ponds, to breed, only to find that these often flooded areas are occupied by a housing development). ▪ Note strategies we can adopt to help animals survive in our community (e.g., relocating snowy owls that pose a threat to themselves and aircraft; turning off architectural and window lighting overnight during migration seasons; finding and documenting the locations of vernal pools so that they can be protected).
What product will they generate?	▪ Create pamphlets for their state's Audubon Society, focused on how to coexist with local wildlife. This organization posts "Quick Guides" on their website, focused on advocating for particular species, but Ms. Parkin noticed that they have only a few. Her students will add to the organization's library of Quick Guides, generating their own pamphlets that describe local species (including their adaptions), the dangers these species face, and the strategies to support their survival. Her students will share these pamphlets with the organization, for display at an information center near one of the local wildlife sanctuaries. The society might even post some pamphlets online!

Figure 8.3 Ms. Parkin's Language Production Project for This Knowledge-Building Cycle

Build In Opportunities for Students to Use Target Vocabulary Words

Just as each knowledge-building cycle revolves around the study of a big idea, each cycle is also focused on the study of a corresponding set of target academic words. By academic words, we mean those terms that are used much more frequently in the academic content areas (science, history, geography, mathematics, literary analysis, etc.) than in informal conversations and social settings. In every cycle, we study a small set of academic words—each is useful for talking and writing about the content-based big idea and is conceptually and linguistically complex (Figure 8.4).

Because these academic words are relevant to the cycle's big idea, these words are ripe for use within the context of a language production project; we must explicitly and intentionally support ELs and their peers to do so. Building in supportive opportunities for students to use the target academic vocabulary words can take many forms, for example:

- including target words in the written and oral questions and prompts posed to students around the project
- creating project-planning routines that involve brainstorming how target words might be used to communicate ideas

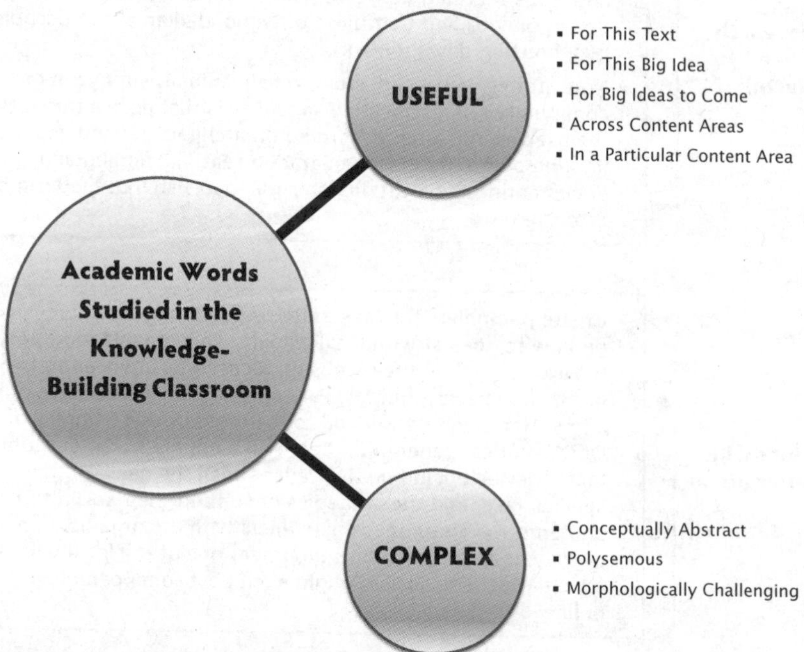

Figure 8.4 Chapter 6 Recap: Target Academic Words Are Useful and Complex

- providing sentence frames that include or beg the use of target words (more on this in the next section)
- modeling the use of target words when carrying out lessons related to the project
- modeling the use of classroom resources that stimulate and support target-word usage (e.g., word wall, word form chart, vocabulary notebook)
- providing checklists or rubrics that prompt students to integrate target words into their projects when revising.

Instructional Tools That Help English Learners Produce Academic Language

Although we often think of these kinds of projects as synonymous with "enrichment" for our highest-performing students, we know that many of our ELs—and their peers—need just the kind of enriching and stimulating learning opportunities that language production projects provide (Halvorsen et al. 2012). And by implementing language production projects as part of a larger instructional approach to building knowledge—an approach made up of the strategies described throughout this book—you are providing your ELs and their peers with the kind of supportive language environment they need to reach your high expectations and produce a content-based written or oral product. But we also know that we need to support them in the process of crafting their projects. For this reason, here we highlight three instructional tools that can be particularly useful to have in your professional "back pocket"—ones that research has shown work well as targeted supports for ELs working toward completing these types of projects (Baker et al. 2014).

Planning and Arranging Content: Graphic Organizers

Venn diagrams, story maps, cause-and-effect charts, and the like have become as commonplace and valued in elementary school classrooms as word walls and pocket charts—and for good reason. These graphic organizers provide a visual, prearranged framework for students to get their ideas on the page and to link these ideas in ways that will ultimately line up with genre and audience expectations (Harris, Graham, and Mason 2006; Kim et al. 2011; Lesaux, Kieffer et al. 2010; Lesaux et al. 2014). These tools are particularly useful to ELs when they are used to facilitate the organization of their ideas into those text structures that are typical of academic texts (see Figure 8.5).

And they work at every level. For example, early in the school year, a first-grade teacher might implement a knowledge-building cycle focused on how we learn and grow, shedding light on how making and learning from mistakes helps our brains develop. As an extended language production project, students could create big books for each of the kindergarten classrooms at their school. In this case, these first-grade authors could communicate about what happens to our brains when we practice and try our best, even when tasks are challenging. Before drafting their pages for the class big book, for example, they might use two graphic organizers: one that supports describing their emerging understanding of the brain and one that helps represent the cause-and-effect text structure to describe a time when they practiced and tried their best, and then as a result, their brains developed.

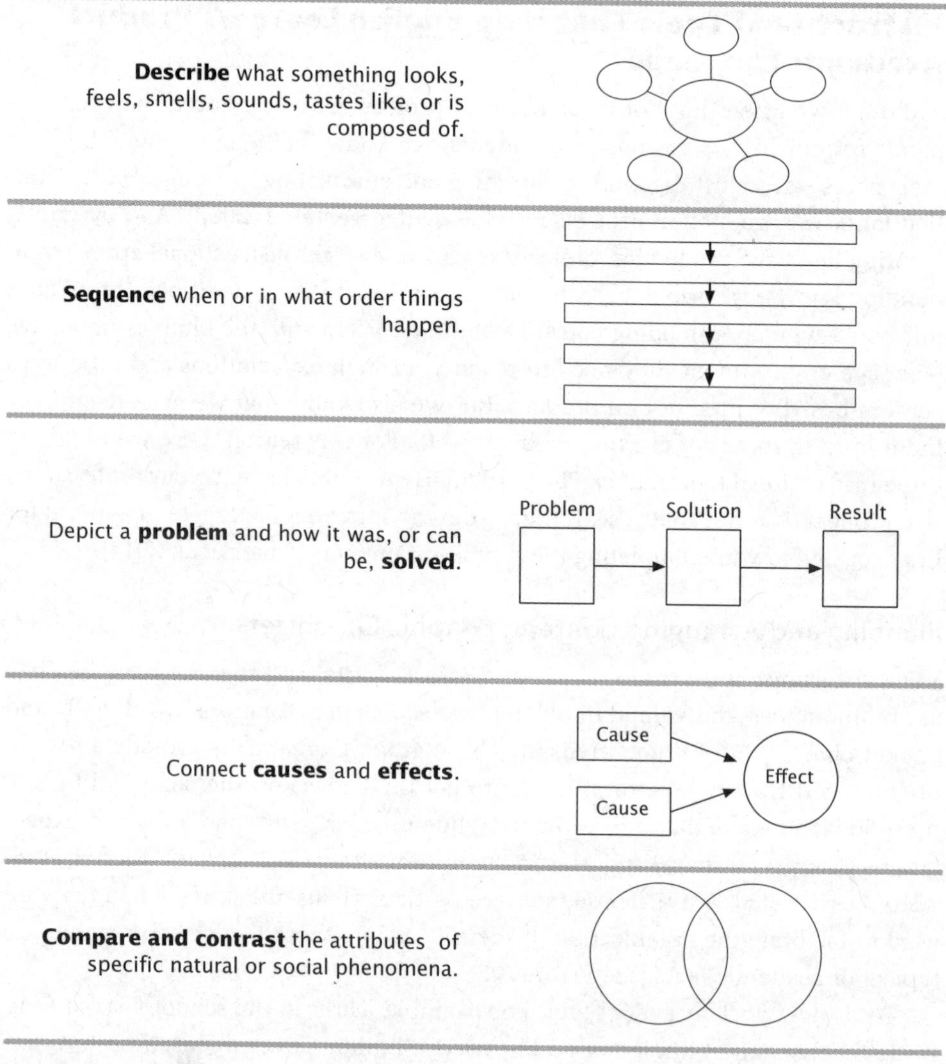

Describe what something looks, feels, smells, sounds, tastes like, or is composed of.
Sequence when or in what order things happen.
Depict a **problem** and how it was, or can be, **solved**.
Problem
Solution
Result
Connect **causes** and **effects**.
Cause
Cause
Effect
Compare and contrast the attributes of specific natural or social phenomena.

Figure 8.5 Common Text Structures and Corresponding Graphic Organizers

Crafting Language: Sentence Starters and Frames

Long a tool in the ESL classroom, sentence starters (e.g., "I learned ______________") and sentence frames (e.g., "I think ____________ because_________") support ELs to take their ideas and put them into academic forms (Kim et al. 2011; Lesaux, Kieffer et al. 2010; Lesaux et al. 2014). Sentence starters and frames can be designed to support students to:

- write or talk about particular content or texts (Figure 8.6)
- craft different parts of a paragraph, such as a topic or concluding sentence
- use the cycle's target academic words accurately
- communicate for different purposes (e.g., rebuttal during debate vs. starting a conversation)
- use connectives to link ideas together.

Often, sentence starters and frames support the use of connectives, which we discuss next.

Tapping Prior Knowledge

"This relates to ______."

"This reminds me of ______."

Making Predictions

"I think ______."

"If ______, then ______."

Summarizing

"The basic gist is ______."

"The key information is ______."

Adopting an Alignment

"The character I most identify with is ______."

"I really got into the story when ______."

"I can relate to this author because ______."

Forming Interpretations

"What this means to me is ______."

"I think this represents ______."

"The idea I am getting is ______."

Revising Meaning

"At first I thought ______, but now I think ______."

"My latest thought about this is ______."

Analyzing the Author's Craft

"I like how the author uses ______ to show ______."

"A golden line for me is ______."

"This word/phrase stands out for me because ______."

Reflecting and Relating

"So the big idea is ______."

"A conclusion I am drawing is ______."

"This relates to my life because ______."

Evaluating

"I like/don't like ______ because ______."

"The most important message is ______ because ______."

From Baker et al. 2014

Figure 8.6 Sample Sentence Starters and Frames for Analyzing Texts

Linking Ideas Together: Supporting Use of Connectives

Connectives (also called *transition* or *signal words*) are words and phrases that link ideas and information within and between sentences; they signal how ideas are related to each other and add logic and reason to the content presented. Having knowledge of connectives is important to support effective reading comprehension, and language production projects provide an opportunity to support the development of this knowledge among ELs (Crosson and Lesaux 2013).

Figure 8.7 presents the types of relationships typically cued by connectives. Connectives include conjunctions, such as *although* and *since*, and adverbs, such as *therefore* and *nonetheless*. Many ELs already understand the concept of communicating relationships between their ideas (e.g., additive, causal, temporal) but tend to rely primarily on more everyday language to express them (e.g., *and*, *because*, and *then*; Crosson et al. 2012).

In the planning and drafting phase of a language production project, supporting ELs' use of connectives will often take the form of sentence starters and frames that integrate these linguistic signposts. For example, when comparing and contrasting the perspectives of an argument, sentence starters might include: "On one hand ________________. However, ________________."

In the revising phases, we can also support ELs' use of connectives, helping them to replace conversational connectives with academic ones. For example, many of our students, ELs and monolingual English speakers alike, use and overuse the connective *and*. We can support students to replace this word with a

Category	Example	Explanation
Additive	During the summer, my mother works in an outdoor food market. *In addition*, she works at a farm.	The relation is considered additive because the two segments are considered equally true, yet there is no direct causal relationship. These relations are typically lists or enumeration.
Temporal	Put on your socks *before* you put on your shoes!	The relationship between two segments is sequential in time.
Causal	I was late to school *because* I missed the bus.	The relation is considered causal because the one segment occurs as a result of the other.
Adversative	Sonia still thinks of Maria as her best friend, *even though* they fight all the time.	Relations are considered adversative when they signal a causal relationship that is in opposition or contrast.

From Crosson and Lesaux 2013

Figure 8.7 Common Categories of Connectives

more precise and academic counterpart (e.g., *in addition*, *moreover*, *likewise*) to support their advanced literacy skill development. Other times, more clearly linking ideas, and using connectives to make these links transparent, will mean that the revision process involves reorganizing the sequence of ideas. In these cases, you could have students cut their compositions up into segments of clauses and then tape them back together—in a new order—with their new connectives. For example, working on a language production project focused on the pros and cons of school dress codes, a student arguing against school uniforms might attempt to portray the alternative perspective, demonstrating an emerging understanding of how to link ideas in academic writing:

> Some students do like to wear uniforms because they get used to them and because they might go to religious schools or private schools.

After conferring with the student, and deciphering his exact reasoning, you might support him to revise his message to the following:

> On the other hand, some students do like to wear uniforms. For example, students who go to religious or private schools wear them all the time, and as a result, get used to them.

Extending Learning Today Prepares English Learners for Opportunities Tomorrow

Punctuating the school year with language production projects extends learning and, in so doing, is a crucial step toward equipping ELs with a sturdy academic foundation. And, just as valuable, these are some of the moments students remember and are most proud of; as today's elementary school students move through the grades, they will stand on this foundation and carry these memories with them. Make no mistake, our ELs will continue to face mounting academic and linguistic demands, but because they engaged in the knowledge-building learning opportunities you provided, they will be better equipped to rise to tomorrow's challenges. The Roman philosopher Seneca noted, "Luck is what happens when preparation meets opportunity." Well, take this book with you to close opportunity gaps and prepare ELs for the opportunities to come. We wish you, and your students, all the luck in the world.

PROTOCOLS FOR PLANNING AND REFLECTION

Planning Language Production Projects

Topic (tied to the cycle's big idea)	
What compelling issue will students focus on?	
What research will they need to undertake?	
What product will they generate?	
What materials and resources will I need to support students' work?	
What instructional tools will I use to support students' academic language use?	

References

Professional Literature Cited

Al Otaiba, S., Y. Petscher, N. Pappamihiel, R. S. Williams, A. K. Dyrlund, and C. Connor. 2009. "Modeling Oral Reading Fluency Development in Latino Students: A Longitudinal Study Across Second and Third Grade." *Journal of Educational Psychology* 101 (2): 315–29.

Alexander, P. A., and T. L. Jetton. 2000. "Learning from Text: A Multidimensional and Developmental Perspective." In *Handbook of Reading Research*, Vol. 3, ed. R. Barr, M. Kamil, P. Mosenthal, and P. D. Pearson, 285–310. New York: Longman.

Armbruster, B., F. Lehr, and J. Osborn. 2001. *Put Reading First: The Research Building Blocks for Teaching Children to Read, K–3*. Washington, DC: National Institute for Literacy.

Aud, S., W. Hussar, G. Kena, K. Bianco, L. Frohlich, J. Kemp, and K. Tahan. 2011. *The Condition of Education 2011* (NCES 2011-033). U. S. Department of Education, National Center for Education Statistics. Washington, DC: U.S. Government Printing Office.

August, D., and K. E. Hakuta. 1997. *Improving Schooling for Language-Minority Children: A Research Agenda.* Washington, DC: National Academy Press.

August, D., and T. Shanahan, eds. 2006. *Developing Literacy in Second-Language Learners: Report of the National Literacy Panel on Language-Minority Children and Youth.* Mahwah, NJ: Lawrence Erlbaum Associates.

Baker, S., N. Lesaux, M. Jayanthi, J. Dimino, C. P. Proctor, J. Morris, R. Gersten, K. Haymond, M. J. Kieffer, S. Linan-Thompson, and R. Newman-Gonchar. 2014. "Teaching Academic Content and Literacy to English Learners in Elementary and Middle School" (NCEE 2014-4012). Washington, DC: National Center for Education Evaluation and Regional Assistance (NCEE), Institute of Education Sciences, U. S. Department of Education. Available at http://ies.ed.gov/ncee/wwc/PracticeGuide.aspx?sid=19.

Ball, E. W., and B. A. Blachman. 1991. "Does Phoneme Awareness Training in Kindergarten Make a Difference in Early Word Recognition and Developmental Spelling?" *Reading Research Quarterly* 26 (1): 49–66.

Bangert-Drowns, R. L., M. M. Hurley, and B. Wilkinson. 2004. "The Effects of School-Based Writing-to-Learn Interventions on Academic Achievement: A Meta-Analysis." *Review of Educational Research* 74 (1): 29–58.

Batalova, J., and M. McHugh. 2010. *Top Languages Spoken by English Language Learners Nationally and by State*. Washington, DC: Migration Policy Institute.

Baumann, J. F., E. C. Edwards, E. M. Boland, S. Olejnik, and E. J. Kame'enui. 2003. "Vocabulary Tricks: Effects of Instruction in Morphology and Context on Fifth-Grade Students' Ability to Derive and Infer Word Meanings." *American Educational Research Journal* 40 (2): 447–94.

Baumann, J. F., D. Ware, and E. C. Edwards. 2007. "Bumping into Spicy, Tasty Words That Catch Your Tongue: A Formative Experiment on Vocabulary Instruction." *The Reading Teacher* 61 (2): 108–22.

Beck, I. L., and M. G. McKeown. 2007. "Increasing Young Low-Income Children's Oral Vocabulary Repertoires Through Rich and Focused Instruction." *The Elementary School Journal* 107 (3): 251–71.

Beck, I. L., M. G. McKeown, and L. Kucan. 2002. *Bringing Words to Life: Robust Vocabulary Instruction*. New York: Guilford Press.

——. 2013. *Bringing Words to Life: Robust Vocabulary Instruction*, 2d ed. New York: Guilford Press.

Beck, I. L., M. G. McKeown, and R. C. Omanson. 1987. "The Effects and Uses of Diverse Vocabulary Instructional Techniques." In *The Nature of Vocabulary Acquisition*, ed. M. G. McKeown and M. E. Curtis, 147–63. Hillsdale, NJ: Lawrence Erlbaum Associates.

Betts, J., S. Bolt, D. Decker, P. Muyskens, and D. Marston. 2009. "Examining the Role of Time and Language Type in Reading Development for English Language Learners." *Journal of School Psychology* 47 (3): 143–66.

Bialystok, E., ed. 1991. *Language Processing in Bilingual Children*. Cambridge, UK: Cambridge University Press.

Bialystok, E., F. I. Craik, and G. Luk. 2012. "Bilingualism: Consequences for Mind and Brain." *Trends in Cognitive Sciences* 16 (4): 240–50.

Blevins, W. 2001. *Teaching Phonics and Word Study in the Intermediate Grades: A Complete Sourcebook*. New York: Scholastic.

Bowers, P. N., J. R. Kirby, and S. H. Deacon. 2010. "The Effects of Morphological Instruction on Literacy Skills a Systematic Review of the Literature." *Review of Educational Research* 80 (2): 144–79.

Cain, K. 2007. "Syntactic Awareness and Reading Ability: Is There Any Evidence for a Special Relationship?" *Applied Psycholinguistics* 28 (4): 679–94.

Cain, K., J. Oakhill, and P. Bryant. 2004. "Children's Reading Comprehension Ability: Concurrent Prediction by Working Memory, Verbal Ability, and Component Skills." *Journal of Educational Psychology* 96 (1): 31–42.

Capps, R., M. Fix, J. Murray, J. Ost, J. S. Passel, and S. Herwantoro. 2005. *The New Demography of America's Schools: Immigration and the No Child Left Behind Act* (Research report). Washington, DC: Urban Institute.

Carlisle, J. F. 2000. "Awareness of the Structure and Meaning of Morphologically Complex Words: Impact on Reading." *Reading and Writing: An Interdisciplinary Journal* 12 (3–4): 169–90.

Carlo, M. S., D. August, B. McLaughlin, C. E. Snow, C. Dressler, D. N. Lippman, and C. E. White. 2004. "Closing the Gap: Addressing the Vocabulary Needs of English-Language Learners in Bilingual and Mainstream Classrooms." *Reading Research Quarterly* 39 (2): 188–215.

Common Core State Standards Initiative. 2010. "Common Core State Standards for the English Language Arts & Literacy in History/Social Studies, Science, and Technical Subjects." Available at www.corestandards.org/ELA-Literacy/.

Coxhead, A. 2011. "The Academic Word List 10 Years On: Research and Teaching Implications." *TESOL Quarterly* 45 (2): 355–62.

Crosson, A. C., and N. K. Lesaux. 2010. "Revisiting Assumptions About the Relationship of Fluent Reading to Comprehension: Spanish-Speakers' Text-Reading Fluency in English." *Reading and Writing* 23 (5): 475–94.

———. 2013. "Connectives: Fitting Another Piece of the Vocabulary Instruction Puzzle." *The Reading Teacher* 67 (3): 193–200.

Crosson, A. C., L. C. Matsumura, R. Correnti, and A. Arlotta-Guerrero. 2012. "The Quality of Writing Tasks and Students' Use of Academic Language in Spanish." *The Elementary School Journal* 112 (3): 469–96.

Cummins, J. 2000. *Language, Power, and Pedagogy: Bilingual Children in the Crossfire*. Clevedon, UK: Multilingual Matters Ltd.

Dale, E. 1965. "Vocabulary Measurement: Techniques and Major Findings." *Elementary English* 42: 82–88.

Deacon, S. H., and J. R. Kirby. 2004. "Morphological Awareness: Just 'More Phonological'? The Roles of Morphological and Phonological Awareness in Reading Development." *Applied Psycholinguistics* 25: 223–38.

Duke, N. K. 2014. *Inside Information: Developing Powerful Readers and Writers of Informational Text Through Project-Based Instruction*. New York: Scholastic.

Duke, N. K., and J. F. Carlisle. 2011. "The Development of Comprehension." In *Handbook of Reading Research*, Vol. 4, ed. M. L. Kamil, P. D. Pearson, E. B. Moje, and P. Afflerbach, 199–228. New York: Routledge.

Duke, N. K., S. Caughlan, M. M. Juzwik, and N. M. Martin. 2012. *Reading and Writing Genre with Purpose in K–8 Classrooms.* Portsmouth, NH: Heinemann.

Duke, N. K., V. Purcell-Gates, L. A. Hall, and C. Tower. 2006. "Authentic Literacy Activities for Developing Comprehension and Writing." *The Reading Teacher* 60 (4): 344–55.

Fry, R. 2007. *How Far Behind in Math and Reading Are English Language Learners?* Washington, DC: Pew Hispanic Center.

Fry, R., and F. Gonzales. 2008. *One-in-Five and Growing Fast: A Profile of Hispanic Public School Students.* Washington, DC: Pew Hispanic Center.

Gándara, P., R. Rumberger, J. Maxwell-Jolly, and R. Callahan. 2003. "English Learners in California Schools: Unequal Resources, Unequal Outcomes." *Education Policy Analysis Archives* 11 (36): 1–54.

García, G. E. 1991. "Factors Influencing the English Reading Test Performance of Spanish-Speaking Hispanic Children." *Reading Research Quarterly* 26 (4): 371–92.

Geva, E., and Z. Yaghoub Zadeh. 2006. "Reading Efficiency in Native English-Speaking and English-as-a-Second-Language Children: The Role of Oral Proficiency and Underlying Cognitive-Linguistic Processes." *Scientific Studies of Reading* 10 (1): 31–57.

Gilbert, J., and S. Graham. 2010. "Teaching Writing to Elementary Students in Grades 4–6: A National Survey." *The Elementary School Journal* 110 (4): 494–518.

Goldenberg, C., R. Gallimore, L. Reese, and H. Garnier. 2001. "Cause or Effect? A Longitudinal Study of Immigrant Latino Parents' Aspirations and Expectations, and Their Children's School Performance." *American Educational Research Journal* 38 (3): 547–82.

Good, R. H., and R. A. Kaminski, eds. 2002. *Dynamic Indicators of Basic Early Literacy Skills*, 6th ed. Eugene, OR: Institute for the Development of Educational Achievement.

Goodwin, A. P., A. C. Huggins, M. S. Carlo, D. August, and M. Calderon. 2013. "Minding Morphology: How Morphological Awareness Relates to Reading for English Language Learners." *Reading and Writing* 26 (9): 1387–415.

Gottardo, A., and J. Mueller. 2009. "Are First- and Second-Language Factors Related in Predicting Second-Language Reading Comprehension? A Study of Spanish-Speaking Children Acquiring English as a Second Language from First to Second Grade." *Journal of Educational Psychology* 101 (2): 330–44.

Graham, S., A. Gillespie, and D. McKeown. 2013. "Writing: Importance, Development, and Instruction." *Reading and Writing* 26 (1): 1–15.

Graham, S., and M. Hebert. 2011. "Writing to Read: A Meta-Analysis of the Impact of Writing and Writing Instruction on Reading." *Harvard Educational Review* 81 (4): 710–44.

Graves, M. F., D. August, and J. Mancilla-Martinez. 2013. *Teaching Vocabulary to English Language Learners*. New York: Teachers College Press.

Grosjean, F. 2010. *Bilingual: Life and Reality*. Cambridge, MA: Harvard University Press.

Guthrie, J. T. 2011. "Best Practices in Motivating Students to Read." In *Best Practices in Literacy Instruction*, 4th ed., ed. L. M. Morrow and L. B. Gambrell, 177–98. New York: Guilford Press.

Halvorsen, A. L., N. K. Duke, K. A. Brugar, M. K. Block, S. L. Strachan, M. B. Berka, and J. M. Brown. 2012. "Narrowing the Achievement Gap in Second-Grade Social Studies and Content-Area Literacy: The Promise of a Project-Based Approach." *Theory & Research in Social Education* 40 (3): 198–229.

Hammer, C. S., S. Scarpino, and M. D. Davison. 2011. "Beginning with Language: Spanish–English Bilingual Preschoolers' Early Literacy Development." In *Handbook of Early Literacy Research*, Vol. 3, ed. S. B. Neuman and D. K. Dickinson, 118–135. New York: Guilford.

Harmon, J. M., K. D. Wood, W. B. Hedrick, J. Vintinner, and T. Willeford. 2009. "Interactive Word Walls: More Than Just Reading the Writing on the Walls." *Journal of Adolescent & Adult Literacy* 52 (5): 398–408.

Harris, K. R., S. Graham, S., and L. H. Mason. 2006. "Improving the Writing, Knowledge, and Motivation of Struggling Young Writers: Effects of Self-Regulated Strategy Development with and Without Peer Support." *American Educational Research Journal* 43 (2): 295–340.

Harris, J. R., and N. K. Lesaux. 2014. Exploring the Reading Comprehension Processes of Adolescent Language Minority Students Who Demonstrate Reading Difficulties. Manuscript submitted for publication.

Hickman, P., S. Pollard-Durodola, and S. Vaughn. 2004. "Storybook Reading: Improving Vocabulary and Comprehension for English-Language Learners." *The Reading Teacher* 57 (8): 720–30.

Jean, M., and E. Geva. 2009. "The Development of Vocabulary in English as a Second Language Children and Its Role in Predicting Word Recognition Ability." *Applied Psycholinguistics* 30 (1): 153–85.

Kelley, J. G., N. K. Lesaux, M. J. Kieffer, and S. E. Faller. 2010. "Effective Academic Vocabulary Instruction in the Urban Middle School." *The Reading Teacher* 64 (1): 5–14.

Kern, L., and N. H. Clemens. 2007. "Antecedent Strategies to Promote Appropriate Classroom Behavior." *Psychology in the Schools* 44 (1): 65–75.

Kieffer, M. J. 2008. "Catching Up or Falling Behind? Initial English Proficiency, Concentrated Poverty, and the Reading Growth of Language Minority Learners in the United States." *Journal of Educational Psychology* 100 (4): 851–68.

———. 2010. "Socioeconomic Status, English Proficiency, and Late-Emerging Reading Difficulties." *Educational Researcher* 39 (6): 484–86.

Kieffer, M. J., G. Biancarosa, and J. Mancilla-Martinez. 2013. "Roles of Morphological Awareness in the Reading Comprehension of Spanish-Speaking Language Minority Learners: Exploring Partial Mediation by Vocabulary and Reading Fluency." *Applied Psycholinguistics* 34 (4): 697–725.

Kieffer, M. J., and N. K. Lesaux. 2007. "Breaking Down Words to Build Meaning: Morphology, Vocabulary, and Reading Comprehension in the Urban Classroom." *The Reading Teacher* 61 (2): 134–44.

———. 2008. "The Role of Derivational Morphology in the Reading Comprehension of Spanish-Speaking English Language Learners." *Reading and Writing* 21 (8): 783–804.

———. 2010. "Morphing into Adolescents: Active Word Learning for English-Language Learners and Their Classmates in Middle School." *Journal of Adolescent & Adult Literacy* 54 (1): 47–56.

———. 2012a. "Development of Morphological Awareness and Vocabulary Knowledge in Spanish-Speaking Language Minority Learners: A Parallel Process Latent Growth Curve Model." *Applied Psycholinguistics* 33 (1): 23–54.

———. 2012b. "Direct and Indirect Roles of Morphological Awareness in the English Reading Comprehension of Native English, Spanish, Filipino, and Vietnamese Speakers." *Language Learning* 62 (4): 1170–204.

Kim, J. S., C. B. Olson, R. Scarcella, J. Kramer, M. Pearson, D. van Dyk, and R. E. Land. 2011. "A Randomized Experiment of a Cognitive Strategies Approach to Text-Based Analytical Writing for Mainstreamed Latino English Language Learners in Grades 6 to 12." *Journal of Research on Educational Effectiveness* 4 (3): 231–63.

Kindle, K. J. 2009. "Vocabulary Development During Read-Alouds: Primary Practices." *The Reading Teacher* 63 (3): 202–11.

Kirby, J. R., S. H. Deacon, P. N. Bowers, L. Izenberg, L. Wade-Woolley, and R. Parrila. 2012. "Children's Morphological Awareness and Reading Ability." *Reading and Writing* 25 (2): 389–410.

Kiuhara, S. A., S. Graham, and L. S. Hawken. 2009. "Teaching Writing to High School Students: A National Survey." *Journal of Educational Psychology* 101 (1): 136–60.

Klingner, J. K., S. Vaughn, M. E. Arguelles, M. T. Hughes, and S. A. Leftwich. 2004. "Collaborative Strategic Reading 'Real-World' Lessons from Classroom Teachers." *Remedial and Special Education* 25 (5): 291–302.

Klingner, J. K., S. Vaughn, A. Boardman, and E. Swanson. 2012. *Now We Get It! Boosting Comprehension with Collaborative Strategic Reading*. San Francisco: Jossey-Bass.

Klingner, J. K., S. Vaughn, and J. S. Schumm, 1998. "Collaborative Strategic Reading During Social Studies in Heterogeneous Fourth-Grade Classrooms." *The Elementary School Journal* 99 (1): 3–22.

Kuhn, M. R., P. J. Schwanenflugel, and E. B. Meisinger. 2010. "Aligning Theory and Assessment of Reading Fluency: Automaticity, Prosody, and Definitions of Fluency." *Reading Research Quarterly* 45 (2): 230–51.

Lawrence, J. F., and C. E. Snow. 2011. "Oral Discourse and Reading." In *Handbook of Reading Research*, Vol. 4, ed. M. L. Kamil, P. D. Pearson, E. B. Moje, and P. Afflerbach, 320–37. New York: Routledge.

Lesaux, N. K. 2010. *Turning the Page: Refocusing Massachusetts for Reading Success.* Boston: Strategies for Children.

——. 2012. "Reading and Reading Instruction for Children from Low-Income and Non-English-Speaking Households." *The Future of Children* 22 (2): 73–88.

Lesaux, N. K., A. Crosson, M. J. Kieffer, and M. Pierce. 2010. "Uneven Profiles: Language Minority Learners' Word Reading, Vocabulary, and Reading Comprehension Skills." *Journal of Applied Developmental Psychology* 31: 475–83.

Lesaux, N. K., J. R. Harris, and P. Sloane. 2012. "Adolescents' Motivation in the Context of an Academic Vocabulary Intervention in Urban Middle School Classrooms." *Journal of Adolescent & Adult Literacy* 56 (3): 231–40.

Lesaux, N. K., M. J. Kieffer, S. E. Faller, and J. G. Kelley. 2010. "The Effectiveness and Ease of Implementation of an Academic Vocabulary Intervention for Linguistically Diverse Students in Urban Middle Schools." *Reading Research Quarterly* 45 (2): 196–228.

Lesaux, N. K., M. J. Kieffer, J. G. Kelley, and J. R. Harris. 2014. "Effects of Academic Vocabulary Instruction for Linguistically Diverse Adolescents Evidence from a Randomized Field Trial." *American Educational Research Journal* 51 (6): 1159–94. doi:10.3102/0002831214532165.

Lesaux, N. K., K. Koda, L. S. Siegel, and T. Shanahan. 2006. "Development of Literacy of Language Minority Learners." In *Developing Literacy in a Second Language: Report of the National Literacy Panel*, ed. D. L. August and T. Shanahan, 75–122. Mahwah, NJ: Lawrence Erlbaum Associates.

Lesaux, N. K., A. A. Rupp, and L. S. Siegel. 2007. "Growth in Reading Skills of Children from Diverse Linguistic Backgrounds: Findings from a Five-Year Longitudinal Study." *Journal of Educational Psychology* 9 (4): 821–34.

Lesaux, N. K., and L. S. Siegel. 2003. "The Development of Reading in Children Who Speak English as a Second Language." *Developmental Psychology* 39 (6): 1005–19.

Leider, C. M., C. P. Proctor, R. D. Silverman, and J. R. Harring. 2013. "Examining the Role of Vocabulary Depth, Cross-Linguistic Transfer, and Types of Reading Measures on the Reading Comprehension of Latino Bilinguals in Elementary School." *Reading and Writing* 9: 1459–85.

Lipka, O., and L. S. Siegel. 2007. "The Development of Reading Skills in Children with English as a Second Language." *Scientific Studies of Reading* 11 (2): 105–31.

Lopez, M. H., and G. Velasco. 2011. "Childhood Poverty Among Hispanics Sets Record, Leads Nation." Washington, DC: Pew Hispanic Center. Available at www.pewhispanic.org/2011/09/28/childhood-poverty-among-hispanics-sets-record-leads-nation/.

Mancilla-Martinez, J., and N. K. Lesaux. 2010. "Predictors of Reading Comprehension for Struggling Readers: The Case of Spanish-Speaking Language Minority Learners." *Journal of Educational Psychology* 102 (3): 701–11.

———. 2011. "The Gap Between Spanish Speakers' Word Reading and Word Knowledge: A Longitudinal Study." *Child Development* 82 (5): 1544–60.

Marzano, R. J., and D. J. Pickering. 2005. *Building Academic Vocabulary: Teacher's Manual*. Alexandria, VA: Association for Supervision and Curriculum Development.

Moats, L. C. 2001. *Speech to Print: Language Essentials for Teachers*. Baltimore: Brookes.

———. 2010. *Speech to Print: Language Essentials for Teachers*, 2d ed. Baltimore: Brookes.

Moss, B. 2005. "Making a Case and a Place for Effective Content Area Literacy Instruction in the Elementary Grades." *The Reading Teacher* 59 (1): 46–55.

Nagy, W. E., and R. C. Anderson. 1984. "How Many Words Are There in Printed School English?" *Reading Research Quarterly* 19 (3): 304–30.

Nagy, W. E., R. C. Anderson, and P. A. Herman. 1987. "Learning Word Meanings from Context During Normal Reading." *American Educational Research Journal* 24 (2): 237–70.

Nagy, W., V. Berninger, and R. Abbott. 2006. "Contributions of Morphology Beyond Phonology to Literacy Outcomes of Upper Elementary and Middle School Students." *Journal of Educational Psychology* 98 (1): 134–47.

Nagy, W. E., and E. H. Hiebert. 2011. "Toward a Theory of Word Selection." In *Handbook of Reading Research*, Vol. 4, ed. M. K. Kamil, P. D. Pearson, P. A. Afflerbach, and E. B. Moje, 388–404. New York: Routledge.

Nagy, W., and D. Townsend. 2012. "Words as Tools: Learning Academic Vocabulary as Language Acquisition." *Reading Research Quarterly* 47 (1): 91–108.

Nation, K., and M. J. Snowling. 2000. "Factors Influencing Syntactic Awareness Skills in Normal Readers and Poor Comprehenders." *Applied Psycholinguistics* 21 (2): 229–41.

National Assessment Governing Board. 2012. "Reading Framework for the 2013 National Assessment of Educational Progress." Available at www.nagb.org/content/nagb/assets/documents/publications/frameworks/reading-2013-framework.pdf.

National Center for Education Statistics. 2013. "What Proportion of Student Groups Are Reaching *Proficient*?" U. S. Department of Education, Institute of Education Sciences, National Center for Education Statistics, National Assessment of Educational Progress (NAEP), various years, 1990–2013 Mathematics and Reading Assessments. Available at www.nationsreportcard.gov/reading_math_2013/#/student-groups.

National Council for the Social Studies. 2013. "Notable Social Studies Trade Books for Young People." www.socialstudies.org/system/files/publications/notable/notable2013.pdf.

National Reading Panel. 2000. *Teaching Children to Read: An Evidence-Based Assessment of the Scientific Research Literature on Reading and Its Implications for Reading Instruction* (National Institute of Health Publication No. 00-4769). Washington, DC: National Institute of Child Health and Human Development.

National Research Council. 2012. *A Framework for K–12 Science Education: Practices, Crosscutting Concepts, and Core Ideas*. Washington, DC: The National Academies Press.

National Science Teachers Association. 2014. "About the Books and the Selection Process." Available at www.nsta.org/publications/ostb/ostb2012.aspx.

National Scientific Council on the Developing Child. 2009. "Young Children Develop in an Environment of Relationships." Working Paper No. 1. Available at http://developingchild.harvard.edu/resources/reports_and_working_papers/working_papers/wp1/.

Ouellette, G. P. 2006. "What's Meaning Got to Do with It: The Role of Vocabulary in Word Reading and Reading Comprehension." *Journal of Educational Psychology* 98 (3): 554.

Paris, S. 2005. "Reinterpreting the Development of Reading Skills." *Reading Research Quarterly* 40 (2): 184–202.

Pearson, P. D., E. H. Hiebert, and M. L. Kamil. 2007. "Vocabulary Assessment: What We Know and What We Need to Learn." *Reading Research Quarterly* 42 (2): 282–96.

Perreira, K. M., M. V. Chapman, and G. L. Stein. 2006. "Becoming an American Parent Overcoming Challenges and Finding Strength in a New Immigrant Latino Community." *Journal of Family Issues* 27 (10): 1383–414.

Proctor, C., M. Carlo, D. August, and C. Snow. 2005. "Native Spanish-Speaking Children Reading in English: Toward a Model of Comprehension." *Journal of Educational Psychology* 97 (2): 246–56.

Proctor, C. P., R. D. Silverman, J. R. Harring, and C. Montecillo. 2012. "The Role of Vocabulary Depth in Predicting Reading Comprehension Among English Monolingual and Spanish-English Bilingual Children in Elementary School." *Reading and Writing* 25 (7): 1635–64.

Proctor, C. P., P. Uccelli, B. Dalton, and C. E. Snow. 2009. "Understanding Depth of Vocabulary Online with Bilingual and Monolingual Children." *Reading & Writing Quarterly* 25 (4): 311–33.

RAND Reading Study Group. 2002. *Reading for Understanding: Toward an R&D Program in Reading.* Arlington, VA: RAND Corporation.

Raver, C. C., P. Garner, and R. Smith-Donald. 2007. "The Roles of Emotion Regulation and Emotion Knowledge for Children's Academic Readiness: Are the Links Causal?" In *Kindergarten Transition and Early School Success*, ed. B. Pianta, K. Snow, and M. Cox, 121–48. Baltimore: Brookes.

Reed, D. K. 2012. *Why Teach Spelling?* Portsmouth, NH: RMC Research Corp., Center on Instruction.

Saul, E. W., and D. Dieckman. 2005. "Choosing and Using Information Trade Books." *Reading Research Quarterly* 40 (4): 502–13.

Scarcella, R. 2003. *Academic English: A Conceptual Framework.* Los Angeles: University of California Language Minority Research Institute.

Schilling, S. G., J. F. Carlisle, S. E. Scott, and J. Zeng. 2007. "Are Fluency Measures Accurate Predictors of Reading Achievement?" *Elementary School Journal* 107 (5): 429–48.

Schleppegrell, M. J. 2001. "Linguistic Features of the Language of Schooling." *Linguistics and Education* 12 (4): 431–59.

Scott, J. A., D. Jamieson-Noel, and M. Asselin. 2003. "Vocabulary Instruction Throughout the Day in Twenty-Three Canadian Upper Elementary Classrooms." *Elementary School Journal* 103 (3): 269–83.

Shanahan, T., K. Callison, C. Carriere, N. K. Duke, P. D. Pearson, C. Schatschneider, and J. Torgesen. 2010. "Improving Reading Comprehension in Kindergarten Through 3rd Grade: A Practice Guide" (NCEE 2010-4038). Washington, DC: National Center for Education Evaluation and Regional Assistance, Institute of Education Sciences, U. S. Department of Education. Available at http://files.eric.ed.gov/fulltext/ED512029.pdf.

Shanahan, T., and C. Shanahan. 2008. "Teaching Disciplinary Literacy to Adolescents: Rethinking Content-Area Literacy." *Harvard Educational Review* 78 (1): 40–61.

Silverman, R., and S. Hines. 2009. "The Effects of Multimedia-Enhanced Instruction on the Vocabulary of English-Language Learners and Non-English-Language Learners in Pre-Kindergarten Through Second Grade." *Journal of Educational Psychology* 101 (2): 305.

Snow, C. E. 2010. "Academic Language and the Challenge of Reading for Learning." *Science* 328 (5977): 450–52.

Snow, C., M. Burns, and P. Griffin, eds. 1998. *Preventing Reading Difficulties in Young Children.* Washington, DC: National Academy Press.

Snow, C. E., and P. Uccelli. 2009. "The Challenge of Academic Language." In *The Cambridge Handbook of Literacy*, ed. D. R. Olson and N. Torrance, 112–33. New York: Cambridge University Press.

Solano-Flores, G. 2006. "Language, Dialect, and Register: Sociolinguistics and the Estimation of Measurement Error in the Testing of English Language Learners." *Teachers College Record* 108 (11): 2354–79.

Swanson, H. L., K. Rosston, M. Gerber, and E. Solari. 2008. "Influence of Oral Language and Phonological Awareness on Children's Bilingual Reading." *Journal of School Psychology* 46: 413–29.

Tannenbaum, K. R., J. K. Torgesen, and R. K. Wagner. 2006. "Relationships Between Word Knowledge and Reading Comprehension in Third-Grade Children." *Scientific Studies of Reading* 10 (4): 381–98.

Taylor, B. M., and N. K. Duke, eds. 2013. *Handbook of Effective Literacy Instruction: Research-Based Practice K–8.* New York: Guilford Press.

UNICEF Innocenti Research Centre. 2009. *Children in Immigrant Families in Eight Affluent Countries: Their Family, National, and International Context.* Florence, IT: United Nations Children's Fund.

Wight, V., M. M. Chau, and Y. Aratani. 2010. *Who Are America's Poor Children? The Official Story.* New York: National Center for Children in Poverty.

Wisconsin Department of Public Education. 2013. "Guide to Creating Text Sets for Grades 2–12." Available at http://ela.dpi.wi.gov/sites/default/files/imce/commoncore/docs/15%20Guide%20to%20Creating%20Text%20Sets.pdf.

Zigler, E., W. S. Gilliam, and S. M. Jones. 2006. *A Vision for Universal Preschool Education.* Cambridge, UK: Cambridge University Press.